COMPLETE CHILDREN'S
COOKBOOK

LONDON, NEW YORK, MELBOURNE,
MUNICH, AND DELHI

Project Editor Elizabeth Yeates
Designer Vanessa Hamilton
Special Sales Creative Project Manager
Alison Donovan
Pre-Production Producer Sarah Isle
Producer Katherine Whyte

First published in Great Britain in 2014
by Dorling Kindersley Limited
80 Strand, London WC2R 0RL

Material in this publication was previously published in:
Children's Cookbook (2004), Cookbook for Girls (2008),
Grow It, Cook It (2008), The Children's Baking Book (2009),
How Does My Garden Grow? (2011), How to Cook (2011),
Get Cooking (2012), Cook It Step by Step (2013)

A Penguin Random House Company

Copyright © 2004, 2008, 2009, 2011, 2013, 2014

2 4 6 8 9 7 5 3
003-265607-Apr/2014

This edition produced for:
The Book People Ltd, Hall Wood Avenue,
Haydock, St Helens, WA11 9UL

A CIP catalogue record for this book
is available from the British Library.

ISBN 978-1-4093-5316-4

Printed in China

Discover more at
www.dk.com

COMPLETE CHILDREN'S COOKBOOK

Contents

Breakfast

Soups and salads

Light bites

Main meals

Desserts

Cakes and muffins

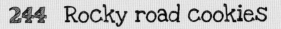

BEFORE
YOU BEGIN

Healthy eating

You need to eat a balanced diet made up of a variety of different foods, so that you can grow, stay healthy, and have lots of energy for life.

Fruits and vegetables

Your body can get important vitamins and minerals, as well as fibre, from fruits and vegetables. Aim to eat about five different portions of these a day. It's useful to think of a portion as roughly equal to the amount you can hold in one hand – such as an apple, a small bunch of grapes, two broccoli florets, or a bowl of salad.

Starchy foods

Bread, cereals, rice, pasta, and potatoes are all starchy foods, also known as carbohydrates. These foods give you energy and should form a part of every meal – whether it's cereal for breakfast, a sandwich lunch, or a pasta dish for dinner. Many starchy foods come in whole-grain varieties, which are healthier for you as they contain more vitamins, minerals, and fibre, when compared with the refined white versions.

Protein

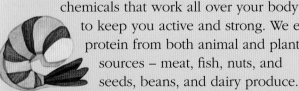

This type of food is made from amino acids, chemicals that work all over your body to keep you active and strong. We eat protein from both animal and plant sources – meat, fish, nuts, and seeds, beans, and dairy produce. It's healthy to eat a variety of these.

Dairy produce

As well as being a source of protein, dairy produce provides valuable vitamins (vitamins A, B12, and D) and minerals (such as calcium). Dairy produce includes milk, yoghurt, cheese, butter, cream, crème fraiche, and cottage cheese. If you're not keen on dairy, then you can get these nutrients in other foods, such as soy milk, tofu, and baked beans.

Fats and sugars

Everyone needs fat for energy and for their bodies to work properly, it's just that it has to be the right type of fat. Fats also help you absorb vitamins and provide essential fatty acids, such as omega-3 and omega-6. Healthy fats (known as polyunsaturated or monounsaturated) are found in vegetable oils, such as sesame, sunflower, soy, and olive, as well as in nuts, seeds, avocados, and oily fish, such as mackerel and salmon. Avoid eating saturated and trans fats (mostly in processed foods).

Sugary foods and salt

Sugar gives you energy and it makes biscuits and cakes taste sweet. Eating too much sugar, though, can lead to mood swings, tooth decay, and obesity. Too much salt is linked with health problems. Avoid very salty snacks and adding too much salt to your cooking.

Weights and measurements

Carefully weigh out the ingredients before you start a recipe. Use measuring spoons, weighing scales, and a measuring jug as necessary. Below are the full names for measurements and their abbreviations.

Metric measures

g = gram

ml = millilitre

Imperial measures

oz = ounce

lb = pound

fl oz = fluid ounce

Spoon measures

tsp = teaspoon

tbsp = tablespoon

Kitchen hygiene

When you're in the kitchen, follow these important rules to keep the germs in check.
- Always wash your hands before you start.
- Wash all fruits and vegetables.
- Any chopping board or knife used in the preparation of raw poultry, meat, or fish should be cleaned thoroughly with hot soapy water before using it again.
- Raw eggs carry a risk of contamination from the salmonella bacterium. Do not give foods with uncooked eggs in them to babies and young children, pregnant women, or the elderly.
- Use separate cutting boards for meat and vegetables.
- Always check the use-by dates on ingredients, and don't use them if the date has passed.

Safety
- Always use oven gloves when handling hot pans, baking trays, and tins.
- Don't put hot pans directly on to the work surface, but use a heat mat, metal rack or trivet, or wooden or heatproof board.
- A sharp knife is safer than a blunt one, but remember that sharp knives should be used carefully and treated with respect.
- Wear an apron to protect your clothes.
- Keep the cooking area clean, and wipe up any spills that could cause accidents.

Cook's notes
- Gather and prepare all ingredients before you start cooking – you don't want to discover halfway through a recipe that you have run out of something important.
- All fruits and vegetables listed in recipes are medium sized unless stated otherwise.
- Use medium-sized eggs unless stated otherwise, and free-range if possible.
- Always use the type of flour specified in a recipe – strong, plain, or self-raising.
- It's important to preheat the oven for 10 minutes or so before using it to allow for the correct temperature to be reached.
- Preparation and cooking times are only a guide. Cooking times may vary according to the type of pan, or oven, and the ripeness of ingredients.
- The easiest way to make cooking stock is using a stock cube, or stock powder, and adding the correct quantity of water, according to instructions on the packet.

Equipment

Here is a handy guide for the equipment used in this book. Each recipe has a tools checklist so that you can gather everything you need before you begin cooking.

Whisk

Kitchen scissors

Pizza cutter

Fork

Peelers

Garlic crusher

Wooden Spoons

Basting brush

Large Spoon

Sharp knife

Table knife

Spoons

Grater

Baking trays

Loaf tin

Non-stick muffin tin

Pizza tray

Cutting boards

Cooling rack

Plastic container

Small bowls

Large bowl

Colander

Glass bowls

Wok

Milk pan

Food processor

Chopping board

Piping bag

Glass jar

Masher

Electric whisk

Food blender

Spatula

Plastic spatula

Ladle

Skewers

Measuring Spoons

Sieve

Egg cup

Slotted Spoon

Spaghetti claw

Ice cream Scoop

Measuring jug

Pastry cutter

Ramekin

Lemon juicer

Cookie cutters

Sandwich cake tin

Glass jugs

Rolling pin

Baking parchment

Square cake tin

Foil

Oven dish

Ceramic flan dish

Lasagne dish

Metal flan dish

Cling film

Stock pot

Frying pan

Small casserole dish

Saucepan with lid

Griddle pan

Ways to cook

Some foods are best cooked at a low heat for a long time, while others respond best to a fast blast of heat. The different techniques shown below are used in different recipes to bring out the best flavours and textures of a dish.

Boil

With the heat turned up high, a liquid will bubble vigorously when boiling.

Simmer

With the heat on low, a mixture will bubble gently when simmering.

Fry

Drizzle some oil into a wide pan to fry food; it's also known as sautéing.

Stir-fry

On a high heat and using oil, stir-frying cooks fast and needs lots of stirring.

Grill
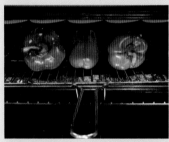
With the heat coming from above, you need to turn food during grilling.

Griddle

On a high heat, a griddle pan's ridges put smoky stripes on the food.

Bake

Cooking food in an oven is baking. Bread, biscuits, cakes, and pies are baked.

Roast

Cooking meat, fish, or vegetables in the oven is known as roasting.

Steam

Placing food above boiling water uses the steam to cook it.

Poach

Cooking in a simmering liquid, such as water or milk, is called poaching.

Deep-fry

Completely immersing food in hot oil is known as deep-frying.

BBQ

Food can be roasted or grilled on a BBQ using heat from charcoal.

Preparing ingredients

Before you start cooking you'll need to get all your ingredients ready. Depending on your recipe, you may have a lot of prep or very little to do.

Dice

To dice an onion, first slice it (while keeping it together) and then slice it at right angles to create small squares or dice. For a courgette, first cut into chunky sticks and then cut across these to make dice.

Chop

Claw Hold the food using a "claw" shape to keep fingers clear of the knife.

Bridge Form a bridge between thumb and finger and cut beneath the bridge.

Peel

Whatever you're peeling, hold the food in one hand and peel away from your body. Carrots are easily peeled from top to bottom but apples can be peeled in one beautiful spiral – with practice. And watch out for your fingers, peelers are sharp.

Grate

As the food passes over the grater's teeth, slithers are forced through.

Mash

Cooked root vegetables can be pushed through a masher until smooth.

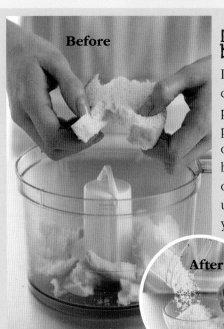

Before

After

Make breadcrumbs

It's quickest done in a food processor. Tear pieces of dried-out bread into the bowl, pop the lid on, and whizz until crumbed. Or, you could grate chunks of the bread instead.

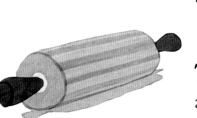

Ways to bake

To get cakes to rise, make light meringue,

and perfect your pastry and biscuits, there are certain techniques in baking that you'll need to master. Once you know what's what you'll be a baking expert!

Sift

Shaking flour or icing sugar through a sieve gets rid of lumps and adds air.

Fold

1. Use a spatula to gently mix while keeping the air in the mixture.

2. Go around the edge of the bowl and then "cut" across, lifting as you go.

Beat

Make a smooth, airy mixture by working fast with a wooden spoon.

Separate an egg

1. Break the shell: tap the egg on the side of the bowl and open up.

2. Transfer the yolk from one shell to the other; put the yolk in another bowl.

Whisk egg whites

1. Mix in a lot of air into a mixture using an electric or a handheld whisk.

2. The mixture should be stiff; if you overwhisk the mixture will collapse.

Rub in

1. Many recipes mix fat (diced butter) and flour using this method.

2. Using your fingertips, pick up the mixture, break up the lumps, and let it fall.

3. Keep rubbing your thumb along your fingertips. To check you've got rid of all the lumps of butter, shake the bowl and any lumps will pop up to the surface.

Make a piping bag

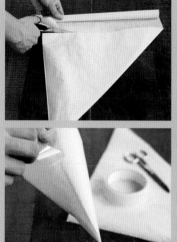

1. Cut a square of greaseproof paper or baking parchment.
2. Fold the paper round on itself to form a cone with a pointy end. Tape in place.

3. Snip off the end of the cone for the icing or cream to come out: for a fine line use a tiny cut; cut higher up the cone for a chunky line.

Cream

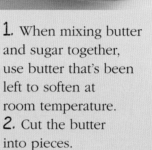

1. When mixing butter and sugar together, use butter that's been left to soften at room temperature.
2. Cut the butter into pieces.

3. Using an electric whisk or a wooden spoon, beat the butter and sugar together until it's paler in colour, light, and fluffy.

Knead

1. Use the heel of your hand to push the bread dough away from you.

2. Fold the squashed end of dough over and turn the whole lot round.

3. Repeat the squashing, folding, and turning motions until the dough is silky soft and smooth. Now the dough is ready to prove.

Roll out

On a floured surface, push down on a rolling pin to make a large flat piece.

Grease a tin

Use some baking paper to spread a thin layer of butter all over the tin.

Line a tin

1. Draw around your tin and add some extra for the paper to go up the sides.

2. Position the paper in the tin. Fold at the corners and snip off any extra bits.

Cooking rules

All recipes should be made under adult supervision. Cooking is great fun, but there are certain rules that you need to know before you begin.

Key to Symbols used in the recipes

How many people the dish serves, or how many portions it makes.

Preparation time, including chilling, freezing, and marinating.

Cooking time A few recipes, such as the salads, don't have this symbol.

⚠ Safety in the kitchen
Take extra care when using electrical equipment, and when this symbol appears, as hot ovens or sharp implements are used.

Getting started
1. Read a recipe all the way through before you start.
2. Wash your hands, put on an apron and tie back your hair.
3. Make sure you have all the ingredients and equipment before you begin a recipe.

Other useful terms

- **Toast** to make a food, such as bread or nuts, crisp, hot, and brown.
- **Purée** a thick pulp of vegetables or fruit blended till smooth in a liquidizer or pushed through a sieve.
- **Marinate** to mix food with a combination of oil, wine, or vinegar with herbs or spices to add flavour.
- **Blend** to mix together so you can't see any of the individual ingredients.
- **Knock back** bash out the excess air when bread dough has risen, before letting it prove.
- **Drizzle** pouring a little stream of liquid, such as olive oil, in tiny drops.
- **Season** adding salt and pepper.

- **Toss** mix some dry ingredients in some wet ingredients, such as lettuce leaves in salad dressing or pasta shapes in a sauce.
- **Reduce to thicken** heating a sauce gently until some of its water is lost (as steam) and the amount of sauce becomes less.
- **Baste** to coat food with meat juice, a marinade or butter, while cooking.

Estimated preparation and cooking times help you to plan your meals.

The ingredients are pictured to help you find them, but remember, they do not show the exact quantities!

Step-by-step pictures and explanations help you to follow the recipes.

Variation and tip boxes suggest different ingredients you can use in the dish and how to ensure it tastes perfect.

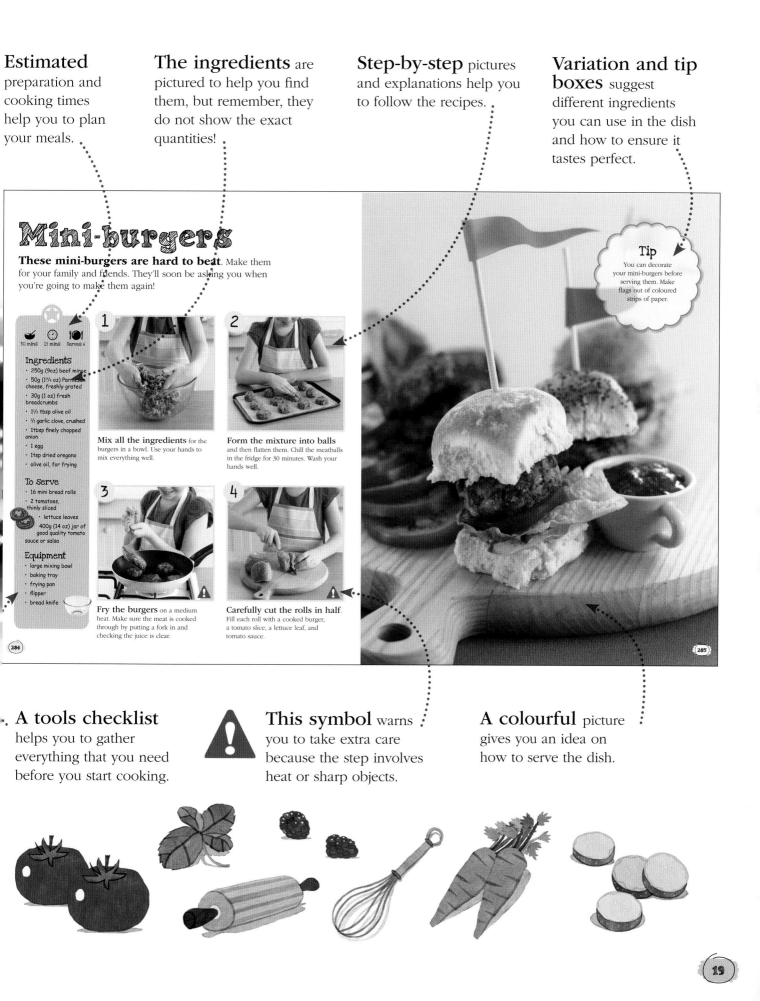

Mini-burgers

These mini-burgers are hard to beat. Make them for your family and friends. They'll soon be asking you when you're going to make them again!

30 mins   15 mins   Serves 6

Ingredients
- 250g (9oz) beef mince
- 50g (1¾ oz) Parmesan cheese, freshly grated
- 30g (1 oz) fresh breadcrumbs
- 1½ tbsp olive oil
- ½ garlic clove, crushed
- 1 tbsp finely chopped onion
- 1 egg
- 1 tsp dried oregano
- olive oil, for frying

To Serve
- 16 mini bread rolls
- 2 tomatoes, thinly sliced
- lettuce leaves
- 400g (14 oz) jar of good quality tomato sauce or salsa

Equipment
- large mixing bowl
- baking tray
- frying pan
- flipper
- bread knife

1 Mix all the ingredients for the burgers in a bowl. Use your hands to mix everything well.

2 Form the mixture into balls and then flatten them. Chill the meatballs in the fridge for 30 minutes. Wash your hands well.

3 Fry the burgers on a medium heat. Make sure the meat is cooked through by putting a fork in and checking the juice is clear.

4 Carefully cut the rolls in half. Fill each roll with a cooked burger, a tomato slice, a lettuce leaf, and tomato sauce.

Tip
You can decorate your mini-burgers before serving them. Make flags out of coloured strips of paper.

204

205

A tools checklist helps you to gather everything that you need before you start cooking.

This symbol warns you to take extra care because the step involves heat or sharp objects.

A colourful picture gives you an idea on how to serve the dish.

BREAKFAST

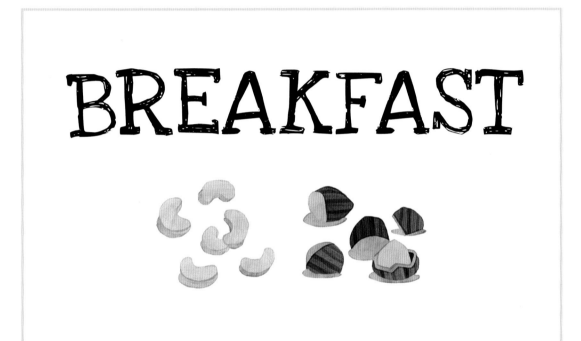

Fruit smoothie

Smoothies are easy to make and taste delicious at any time of day. Follow these four simple steps for a burst of fruity goodness.

10 mins   Serves 2-4

Ingredients
- 1 ripe banana
- 200g (7oz) ripe strawberries
- 200ml (7fl oz) milk
- 1tbsp of clear runny honey
- 100ml (3½fl oz) natural yoghurt

Equipment
- sharp knife
- chopping board
- measuring spoons
- blender

Rinse and drain the strawberries in cold water and then hull them by holding the pointed end and slicing off the stem.

Cut the strawberries in half and put them to one side. Peel the banana and throw away the skin. Slice the banana, for easy blending in step 4.

Carefully put the banana and strawberries into the blender. Add the milk, yoghurt, and honey and put the lid on securely.

Blend the mixture until it is completely smooth. Pour the smoothie into tall glasses and enjoy – what a great way to start the day!

Griddled fruit and honey

You will love this fruit griddled – it helps bring out the sweetness. If you don't have a griddle pan, place the fruit under a hot grill.

1

Cut each peach in half and remove the stone. Then cut each into quarters. Halve the apricots and remove the stones.

2

In a large bowl, mix together the sugar and cinnamon, then add the fruit. Toss to coat in the sugar mixture.

3

Preheat a griddle pan and add the peaches, flesh side down. Cook for 2 to 3 minutes. Add the apricots, and turn over the peaches. Cook until caramelised.

4

Meanwhile, place the yoghurt in a bowl and pour over the honey. Stir to create a rippled effect. Serve the warmed griddled fruit with the yoghurt and honey dip.

10 mins 6 mins Serves 4

Ingredients
- 3 peaches
- 4 apricots
- 2 tbsp caster sugar
- 1/2 tsp ground cinnamon
- 200ml (7fl oz) Greek yoghurt
- 2 tbsp clear honey

Equipment
- knife
- chopping board
- 2 mixing bowls
- 2 metal spoons
- griddle pan
- tongs

Fruity cereal

5 mins   20 mins   Serves 8

You need a hearty breakfast to keep you going through the morning. This delicious cereal will keep you filled up until snack time. You can try using dried cranberries instead of raisins.

Ingredients

- 2tbsp sunflower oil
- 6tbsp golden syrup or runny honey
- 350g (12oz) rolled oats
- 115g (4oz) hazelnuts
- 60g (2oz) pumpkin seeds
- 115g (4oz) dried banana chips, broken into small pieces
- 115g (4oz) raisins
- milk or plain yoghurt to serve

Equipment

- large saucepan
- wooden spoon
- large bowl
- baking tray
- oven gloves
- airtight container to store cereal in afterwards

Ask an adult to preheat the oven to 200°C (400°F/Gas 6). Heat the oil and golden syrup or honey in a saucepan over a low heat.

Pour the golden syrup and oil mixture into a large bowl with the oats, hazelnuts, and pumpkin seeds.

Place the mixture onto a baking tray, spread it out, and cook in the oven for 10 minutes or until the cereal turns a golden brown colour.

Let the oat mixture cool down on the tray and then tip it into a bowl. Add the dried banana chips and raisins to the mixture and stir well.

5

Serve your cereal in a bowl with milk or a spoonful of plain yoghurt.

Sticky stuff

The sugar and golden syrup act like a glue in this recipe. They help the dry ingredients to stick together, making the muesli bars incredibly chewy and sticky!

Fruit bars

Cereal bars are perfect for breakfast or as a snack. Once you've mastered this recipe, experiment with other fruit and nuts.

15 mins   30 mins   Serves 12

Ingredients

- 115g (4oz) unsalted butter
- 100g (3½oz) light brown sugar
- 115g (4oz) golden syrup or runny honey
- 300g (10oz) rolled oats
- 100g (3½oz) raisins
- 50g (1¾oz) mixed nuts, chopped

Equipment

- 30 x 23 x 4cm (12 x 9 x 1½in) baking tin
- baking paper
- wooden spoon
- saucepan

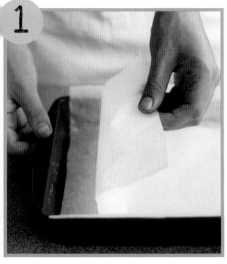

1 **Preheat the oven** to 150°C (300°F/Gas 2). Grease your baking tin then line it with 2 sheets of baking paper.

2 **Melt the butter,** sugar, and golden syrup (or runny honey) in a saucepan over a low heat.

3 **Place all the other** ingredients in a large bowl and pour in the sugar mixture.

4 **Spread the mixture** evenly in the baking tin and, using a masher, press it down firmly so it sticks together. Bake for 20–30 minutes or until golden brown.

5 **When the muesli bars** are baked, leave them to cool for 5 minutes. Then, using a cloth to hold the tin, cut them into 12 squares. Remove them from the tin when fully cooled and firm.

Eggy bread

Popular around the world, this dish is eaten in Portugal at Christmas and in Spain and Brazil at Easter.

10 mins | 10 mins | Serves 2

Ingredients

- 4 large eggs
- 240ml (8fl oz) milk
- ¼tsp ground cinnamon
- 4 slices thick white bread, cut into triangles
- 2tbsp sunflower oil
- 100g (3½oz) blueberries
- maple syrup, to serve

Equipment

- whisk
- mixing bowl
- shallow dish
- frying pan and spatula

1

Crack the eggs into a mixing bowl. Add the milk and cinnamon and whisk together.

2

Pour the mixture into a shallow dish. Soak the bread in the mixture for about 30 seconds.

3

Heat half a tablespoon of the oil in a frying pan on a low heat. Carefully place two triangles in the pan.

4

Fry the triangles on both sides until they turn golden. Repeat steps 3 and 4 for the remaining bread triangles.

5

Serve the eggy bread warm, with blueberries and maple syrup or try it with butter and jam.

Four ways with eggs

Eggs are perfect for breakfast as they're packed with goodness to start your day. You can try cooking eggs in different ways to vary your breakfast.

Scrambled eggs with bacon

The secret to scrambled eggs is not to overcook them as otherwise they will become dry and rubber.

Ingredients

This recipe is for 1 person. It takes 2 minutes to prepare and 8 minutes to cook.

- 1 slice of streaky bacon
- 1 tbsp milk
- 1 egg
- a small knob of butter
- pinch of dried basil
- 1 slice of buttered toast

Method

- Ask an adult to grill the bacon. When it's cooked use a knife and fork to cut it up into small pieces.
- Whisk together the milk and egg until creamy.
- Melt the butter in a frying pan on a medium heat and add the egg and milk mixture. Stir often until the eggs are just cooked, but still creamy. Mix in the grilled bacon pieces.

Boiled eggs

How do you like your boiled egg? Look at the options below and decide how long to cook your egg for.

Ingredients

This recipe is for 1 person. It takes 2 minutes to prepare and 4-8 minutes to cook.

- 1 egg
- 1 piece of buttered toast, sliced

Method

- Fill a small saucepan with water and lower one egg into it. Ask an adult to boil the water. When the water has boiled, lower the temperature and let it simmer.
- SOFT BOILED
Cook for four minutes. This egg will have a soft, runny yolk - perfect for dipping your slices of toast into!
- MEDIUM BOILED
Cook for six minutes. The egg yolk will be medium-firm.
- HARD BOILED
Cook for eight minutes. The yolk will be really firm.

Make your own

The eggs of many different types of birds can be eaten, but those of the female chicken (hens) are most common and are widely available.

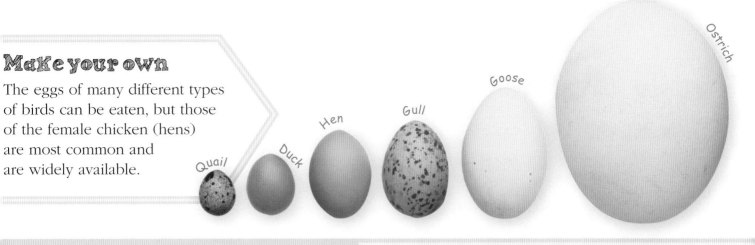

Quail

Duck

Hen

Gull

Goose

Ostrich

3

Fried eggs

If you like your egg yolk to be runny, then fry the egg on one side only. If you prefer them well-done, fry on both side.

Ingredients

This recipe is for 1 person. It takes 1 minute to prepare and 2-4 minutes to cook.

· 1 tsp sunflower oil

· 1 egg

· 1 slice of buttered toast

· ground black pepper, to season

Method

• Ask an adult to heat the oil in a pan over a medium heat.

• Crack the egg into a bowl. If any of the shell falls into the bowl scoop it out using a spoon. Gently tip the egg into the frying pan.

• The egg needs to be fried for about two minutes on a medium heat. If you like your eggs well-done, carefully flip the egg with a spatula.

• Serve the fried egg on a slice of toast. Season with black pepper.

4

Poached eggs

Poaching eggs can be tricky, but keep practising and you will soon master the technique to create a perfect poached egg.

Ingredients

This recipe is for 1 person. It takes 5 minutes to prepare and 2-4 minutes to cook.

· 1 egg

· 1 slice of buttered toast

Method

• Fill a large saucepan with water and ask an adult to boil the water. When the water has boiled, lower the temperature so the water is barely boiling.

• Crack the egg into a cup and carefully tip the egg into the water.

• The egg needs to be poached for about 2 minutes or until the white is set.

• Carefully remove the egg with a slotted spoon and place on a piece of kitchen towel to drain.

• Serve on a slice of buttered toast.

Potato rösti

This classic Swiss dish is made from grated potatoes that are fried until crispy. You can make big pan-sized röstis, but these smaller pancakes are easier to turn. Eat them for breakfast, or as a side dish to a main meal.

20 mins | 10-20 mins | Makes 8

Ingredients

- 3-4 medium-sized floury potatoes, about 800g (1¾lb), peeled
- salt and freshly ground black pepper
- 4tbsp olive oil

Equipment

- saucepan
- colander
- grater
- bowl
- clean tea towel
- fork
- large frying pan
- metal spoon
- flipper

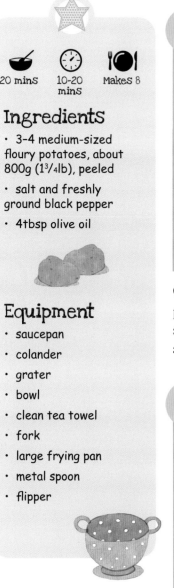

Cut the potatoes in half and parboil them in a saucepan of boiling salted water for 6–7 minutes. Drain and allow to cool.

Carefully coarsely grate the potatoes into a bowl or onto a plate – graters with big holes are best. Transfer the potato to a clean tea towel.

Use the tea towel to squeeze out any excess liquid, which would make the rösti soggy. Add the salt and pepper, and mix lightly with a fork.

Heat half the oil in a large frying pan and let it begin to sizzle. Shape spoonfuls of the grated potato mixture into round cakes 1–2cm (½–¾in) thick and place four cakes into the pan.

5

Gently fry the rösti

for about 5–10 minutes, or until golden brown and crisp underneath. Turn them with a spatula or fish slice, then cook for a further 5–10 minutes, or until browned on the other side. Remove from the pan and keep warm while cooking the rest of the mixture in the remaining oil.

Variation

Get inventive and mix the potato with some other delicious root vegetables, such as sweet potatoes, carrots, parsnips, or even beetroot.

Breakfast omelette

This omelette is a tasty variation of a traditional breakfast fry-up. It has all the right ingredients for a filling weekend brunch – eggs, bacon, tomato, mushrooms – and could even be served with a green salad as a light or main meal.

10 mins   15 mins   Serves 1

Ingredients

- 2 eggs
- 2tbsp of milk
- 30g (1oz) cheddar cheese
- a knob of unsalted butter
- salt and pepper

For the filling

- 1 tomato
- 2 rashers of bacon
- 1tsp of sunflower oil
- 60g (2oz) mushrooms

Equipment

- whisk
- jug
- grater
- wooden spoon
- sharp knife
- 2 chopping boards
- small non-stick frying pan or omelette pan
- wooden spatula
- 2 plates
- kitchen paper

Whisk the eggs and milk together in a jug. (This will make it easy to pour in step 5.) Grate the cheese and stir it in to the egg mixture. Season.

Cut the tomato into chunks and slice the mushrooms. On a separate board, remove the rind from the bacon and cut the meat into cubes.

Place the frying pan over a medium heat and fry the bacon for 3 minutes or until cooked completely. Tip the bacon onto a plate, lined with kitchen paper.

Heat the oil and fry the mushrooms for 2 minutes. Add the tomato to the pan and cook for 1 minute. Put the tomato and mushrooms onto a plate.

5 **Melt the butter** in the pan. Pour in the egg so that it covers the base of the pan. Cook the egg on a medium heat until the edges begin to cook and set.

6 **Using a spatula**, push the cooked egg into the centre of the pan. The uncooked egg will run to the sides. Repeat until all the egg is cooked.

7 **Shake the pan** to release the omelette and spoon the filling over one half. Slide the omelette out onto a plate and gently flip the unfilled half over the top.

Pancakes

Ingredients

- 1 egg
- 110g (3³/₄ oz) self-raising flour
- 1tsp bicarbonate of soda
- 150ml (5fl oz) milk
- sunflower oil for frying
- 200g (7oz) fresh strawberries
- 4tbsp plain yoghurt

Equipment

- mixing bowl
- measuring jug
- whisk
- frying pan
- tablespoon
- flipper

Pancakes can be thick or thin depending on the ingredients you use to make them. Have fun trying out both types of pancake. Thin pancakes are often called "crêpes". Make this dish for your family.

Wash the strawberries and cut a few of them into halves and place to one side (they will be used for decoration). Hull the remaining strawberries and carefully cut into slices.

Put the egg, flour, bicarbonate of soda, and milk into a bowl. Whisk up the mixture until it's smooth.

Heat a tablespoon of sunflower oil in a frying pan. Use a large spoon to carefully pour the pancake mixture into the pan. Fry the pancake until golden brown in the bottom.

Flip the pancake and fry the other side. Place a few strawberry slices and a tablespoon of yoghurt on a pancake, then a pancake on top. Repeat until you have a two layers of strawberries.

Tip

Put half the muffins in an airtight container and place in the freezer to have at a later date. The muffins can stay in the freezer for up to two months.

Blueberry muffins

Muffins make a delicious dessert. The blueberries make the muffins extra moist and yummy. They pop while they cook to make great bursts of colour.

Preheat the oven to 200°C (400°F/ Gas 6). Line a 12-cup muffin tin with muffin cases. Melt the butter in a pan, then set aside to cool. Sift the flour into a bowl, mix in the baking powder, sugar, zest.

Make a well in the centre of the flour. Mix the yoghurt, eggs, and cooled melted butter together in a large jug, then pour into the dry ingredients.

Add the blueberries. Mix until just combined, but don't over-mix or the muffins will be heavy.

Spoon evenly into the muffin cases and bake for 20 minutes, or until golden and springy. Cool in the tin for five minutes.

15 mins 20 mins Serves 12

Ingredients

- 50g (1¾oz) unsalted butter
- 250g (9oz) self-raising flour
- 1tsp baking powder
- 75g (2½oz) caster sugar
- finely grated zest of 1 lemon (optional)
- 250ml (8fl oz) plain yoghurt
- 2 large eggs, lightly beaten
- 250g (9oz) blueberries

Equipment

- mixing bowl
- sieve
- large jug
- wooden spoon
- 2 dessert spoons
- 12-cup muffin tin and muffin cases

10 mins · 25 mins · Serves 10

Ingredients

- 250g (9oz) plain flour
- 1tbsp baking powder
- 100g (3½oz) porridge oats
- 125g (4oz) ready-to-eat dried apricots (chopped)
- 50g (2oz) soft light brown sugar
- ½tsp salt
- 2 medium eggs (beaten)
- 175ml (6floz) milk
- 75ml (3floz) sunflower oil
- 5tbsp clear honey

Equipment

- 2 x 6-hole or 12-hole muffin tin
- 10 paper muffin cases
- large mixing bowl
- sieve
- wooden spoon
- large jug
- fork
- oven gloves
- cooling rack

Oat and honey muffins

These fluffy light muffins are perfect for breakfast or a mid-morning snack because they are packed with nutritious oats and dried fruit.

Preheat the oven to 375°F (190°C/Gas 5). Line a muffin tin with 10 paper cases. Sift the flour and baking powder into a bowl and stir in the oats, apricots, sugar, and salt.

Put the flour mixture to one side. In a large jug, beat together the eggs, milk, oil, and honey with a fork until thoroughly mixed and frothy.

Pour the wet mixture in the jug over the dry ingredients in the bowl. Stir with a wooden spoon until the ingredients are just combined. The batter will be lumpy and quite runny.

Divide the mixture between the muffin cases, so they are two-thirds full and cook on the top shelf of the oven for 20–25 minutes. Leave in the tin for a few minutes, then transfer to a cooling rack.

Variation

Don't like apricots? Just replace them with your favourite dried fruit, such as papaya or mango.

SOUPS AND SALADS

Tomato soup

Soup is a comforting meal or snack

and makes an easy starter to a main meal. This soup is wonderfully thick and creamy and is topped with small pieces of toast, called croutons.

20 mins   35 mins   Serves 2-4

Ingredients

- 1 small onion
- 1 small carrot
- 4tbsp olive oil
- 1 garlic clove, crushed
- 1tbsp plain flour
- 400g (14oz) can chopped tomatoes
- 1tbsp tomato purée
- 1tsp fresh thyme leaves (optional)
- 450ml (15fl oz) vegetable stock
- a pinch of sugar
- a squeeze of lemon juice
- 2 thick slices of bread
- salt and pepper

Equipment

- sharp knife
- peeler
- chopping board
- medium saucepan
- wooden spatula
- bread knife
- non-stick baking tray
- oven gloves
- ladle
- blender

1 **Peel and chop** the onion and carrot. Ask an adult to preheat the oven to 220°C (425°F/Gas 7). Heat half the olive oil in the saucepan, over a medium heat.

2 **Add the onion** and carrot and cook for about 5 minutes to soften, stirring occasionally. Stir in the garlic and flour and cook the mixture for 1 minute.

3 **Add the tomatoes,** purée, thyme, stock, sugar, and lemon juice and bring to a boil. Reduce the heat and simmer for 20–25 minutes. Remove from the heat and cool.

4 **While the soup** is cooking, use cookie cutters to cut out shapes for the croutons. Scatter the bread on the baking tray, drizzle over the remaining olive oil.

5 **Use your hands** to coat the bread in the oil and season. Bake for 8–10 minutes, until crisp and golden. Turn after about 4 minutes for even cooking.

6 **Ladle the cool soup** into the blender, and blend until smooth. Rehear in a saucepan, then ladle into bowls. Serve with the croutons on top.

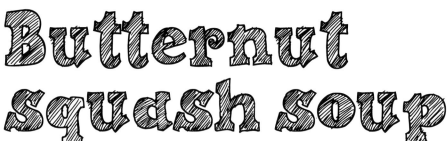

Butternut Squash Soup

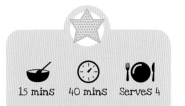

15 mins   40 mins   Serves 4

Ingredients

- 1kg (2¼lb) butternut squash
- 1tbsp vegetable oil
- 1 onion (chopped)
- 600ml (1 pint) hot vegetable stock
- 2tbsp honey

To serve
- French stick
- Gruyére or Swiss cheese
- freshly chopped parsley

Equipment

- tablespoon
- peeler
- baking tray
- wooden spoon
- food processor
- large saucepan

This wholesome, warming soup is perfect for a cold day. It's made from roasted butternut squash, but you could also try it with pumpkin if you prefer.

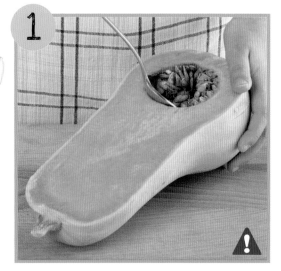

Preheat the oven to 200°C (400°F/ Gas 6). Cut the butternut squash in half lengthwise, then use a spoon to scoop out the seeds and pith.

Cut into large chunks, then, using a peeler, remove the skin. Cut the chunks into 2.5cm (1in) cubes.

Place on a baking tray, season with salt and pepper, then drizzle over the oil. Roast for 20 minutes, then remove from the oven.

Add the onion and stir. Return to the oven and cook for a further 15 minutes. Remove from the oven and allow to cool a little.

Place the butternut squash and onion in a food processor with half of the stock and blend until smooth.

6

Place the purée

in a saucepan with the remaining stock and honey. Simmer for 3 to 4 minutes. Serve with slices of toasted French stick, cheese, and parsley.

Pea and mint soup

This soup can be eaten hot or cold so you can have it all year round! For a different flavour you can add bacon and crème fraiche. Serve with fresh, crusty bread.

10 mins · 5 mins · Serves 4

Ingredients

- 250g (9oz) frozen peas, such as petit pois
- 450ml (15fl oz) hot vegetable stock
- pinch of freshly grated nutmeg
- handful of fresh mint leaves, roughly chopped or 1 tbsp of dried mint
- a few fresh thyme stalks, leaves picked (optional)
- ground black pepper
- 4 slices of crusty bread, to serve

Equipment

- electric kettle
- mixing bowl
- large plate
- large jug
- electric blender
- saucepan

Put the peas in a bowl, then pour over boiling water, cover and leave to stand for about five minutes. Tip into a colander over a sink to drain off the water.

Using a blender, whiz the peas, stock, nutmeg, and herbs until smooth and combined. Add more stock if the soup is too thick. Season well with black pepper.

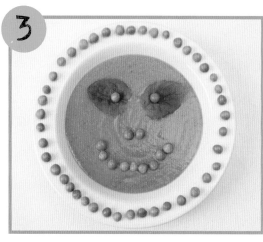

Spoon into cups or serve in a bowl. Have fun and make a face using fresh peas and mint leaves.

Variation

Add one tablespoon of crème fraiche to each portion of soup to make it creamy. If you like streaky bacon then ask an adult to grill four slices. Cut up a slice for each cup of soup.

50

Onion and leek soup

Onions and leeks are great for adding flavour to savoury meals. They also contain vitamins and minerals that will help to keep your heart healthy.

1

Melt the butter in a large saucepan then add the onion and leeks. Cook gently for about 5-7 minutes until the onion and leeks are softened.

2

Add the potatoes and stock. Cook for a further 10 minutes or until the potatoes are tender.

3

Stir in the tarragon. Remove from heat and leave to cool. It is dangerous to blend a soup when hot as the heat will force off the lid of the blender.

4

Pour the cold mixture into a blender. Blend until smooth. Reheat with the milk in a saucepan to make soup. Season with salt and pepper.

10 mins   20 mins   Serves 4

Ingredients

- 50g (2oz) butter
- 4 leeks, trimmed and sliced
- 1 large onion, chopped
- 2 medium potatoes, chopped
- 1 litre (1.7 pints) chicken stock
- small bunch of tarragon, chopped
- 250ml (9fl oz) milk
- salt and pepper
- crème fraîche

Equipment

- chopping board
- sharp knife
- saucepan
- wooden spoon
- electric blender

Noodle soup

This is a healthy, filling, and complete meal in a bowl. Best of all, it only uses one saucepan so there is less to wash up afterwards!

15-20 mins | 15 mins | Serves 2

Ingredients

- 2tsp of vegetable oil
- 2 spring onions (trimmed and sliced diagonally)
- 1 thin slice of fresh ginger, peeled (optional)
- juice of ½ lime
- 600ml (1pt) fish stock made with ⅓ of stock cube)
- 1tsp of soy sauce
- 75g (2½oz) fine egg noodles
- 60g (2oz) baby corn (halved)
- 60g (2oz) sugar snap peas
- 1 drop of sesame oil
- 125g (4oz) ready-to-cook raw prawns (shelled)
- 2tsp of chopped fresh coriander (optional)

Equipment

- medium saucepan
- wooden spoon
- measuring jug

1

Heat the vegetable oil in a medium saucepan. Gently fry the spring onions over a medium heat for 1–2 minutes, or until soft.

2

Stir the ginger, stock, lime juice, and soy sauce into the spring onion and bring to the boil. Lower the heat and then simmer for 2–3 minutes.

3

Remove the ginger. Add the noodles and corn and bring to the boil. After 1½ minutes, add the sugar snap peas and cook for a further 1½ minutes.

4

Lower the heat to bring the soup back to a simmer. Stir in the prawns and cook them for 2–3 minutes, or until pink. Stir in the sesame oil and coriander.

Tip

Do not overcook the prawns because it makes the texture rubbery! And if you are using frozen prawns, make sure that you defrost them completely before cooking them.

Simple soups

Soups can be as simple or involved as you like. Enjoy them as a starter, or serve them with crusty bread and turn them into a meal in themselves.

Pea soup

This vibrant soup is a perfect meal on a cold winter's day. Try adding cubes of grilled bacon, or the pea and mint soup recipe on pages 50–51.

Ingredients

This recipe is for 4 people. It takes 20 minutes to prepare and 15 minutes to cook.

· 4 sliced spring onions, sliced

· 55g (2oz) butter

· 600ml (1 pint) vegetable stock

· 350g (12oz) frozen peas

· 150ml (¼ pint) single cream

· 2tsp chopped fresh mint

Method

● Cook the sliced spring onions in the butter in a saucepan until soft.

● Add the vegetable stock and bring to the boil.

● Add the frozen peas, then simmer for 3–4 minutes. Cool for a few minutes.

● Pour into a blender and whizz until smooth.

● Return the soup to the saucepan and stir in the single cream and chopped fresh mint.

● Simmer gently for 5 minutes. Season with salt and freshly ground black pepper.

Hot tortilla soup

Add some grated cheese to melt into the soup when served. This will make the soup even more delicious. This recipe is for 4 people.

Ingredients

This soup takes 20 minutes to prepare and 20 minutes to cook.

· 1 onion

· 1 garlic clove

· 1 red chilli

· 1tbsp olive oil

· 1tbsp paprika

· 1 litre (1¾ pints) tomato juice

· 300ml (10fl oz) vegetable stock

· 4tbsp sunflower oil

· 2 soft corn tortillas

· 2tbsp fresh coriander

· juice of 1 lime

Method

● Finely chop the onion, garlic and chilli and gently cook in the olive oil until soft.

● Add the paprika, tomato juice, and vegetable stock, and simmer for 15 minutes.

● Heat the sunflower oil in a frying pan, add strips of soft corn tortillas, and fry until crisp. Drain on kitchen paper.

● Stir in chopped fresh coriander and the lime juice, season with salt and freshly ground black pepper and top with the tortillas.

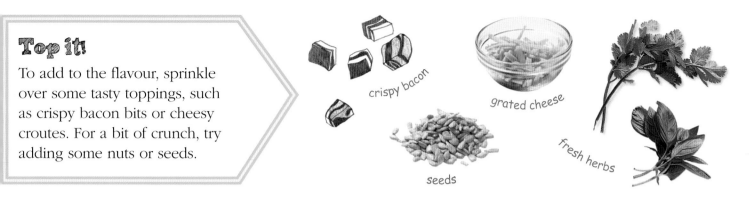

Top it!

To add to the flavour, sprinkle over some tasty toppings, such as crispy bacon bits or cheesy croutes. For a bit of crunch, try adding some nuts or seeds.

crispy bacon

grated cheese

seeds

fresh herbs

3

Corn chowder

Chowder is a thick soup from New England in the USA. You can use fresh, frozen, or tinned sweetcorn here.

Ingredients

This recipe is for 4 people. It takes 15 minutes to prepare and 30 minutes to cook.

· 1 large onion, chopped
· 200g (9oz) sweetcorn
· 1 large carrot, sliced
· 350g (12oz) potatoes, peeled and chopped
· 1tbsp sunflower oil
· 1 bouquet garni (optional)
· 1 bay leaf
· 1.2 litres (2 pints) vegetable stock
· 300ml (10fl oz) milk

Method

● Gently cook the onion in the oil until soft.

● Add the corn, carrot, potatoes, bouquet garni, and bay leaf. Cook for 2 minutes, stirring constantly. Add the stock and bring to the boil.

● Reduce the heat to medium to low. Cover with a lid and cook for 15 minutes, stirring occasionally. Add the milk and cook for a further 5 minutes.

● Scoop out some of the vegetables and blend the rest of the soup until smooth. Return the vegetables and blended soup to the pan and warm through.

4

Spicy lentil soup

This soup easy-to-make and really healthy. Serve it with cheesy croutes or crusty garlic bread.

Ingredients

This recipe is for 4 people. It takes 15 minutes to prepare and 35 minutes to cook.

· 2 onions
· 2 celery sticks
· 2 carrots
· 1tbsp olive oil
· 2 finely chopped garlic cloves
· 1tsp curry powder
· 150g (5½oz) red lentils
· 1.4 litres (2½ pints) vegetable stock
· 120ml (4fl oz) tomato juice

Method

● Gently fry the onions, celery sticks, and carrots – all finely chopped – in the olive oil.

● Cook for 5 minutes, then add the garlic and curry powder, and stir for a further 1 minute.

● Add the lentils, vegetable stock, and tomato juice. Bring to the boil, then reduce the heat, cover, and simmer for 25 minutes.

● Season with salt and freshly ground black pepper and serve straight away.

10 mins   5 mins   Serves 4

Ingredients

- 100g (3½oz) green beans, trimmed and halved
- 100g (3½oz) tenderstem broccoli
- 100g (3½oz) fresh peas
- 150g (5½oz) mixed leaves e.g. baby spinach, rocket and watercress

Dressing

- 2tbsp white wine vinegar
- 2tbsp extra virgin olive oil
- 1tbsp lemon juice
- 1tsp clear honey
- 1tsp pesto sauce

Equipment

- saucepan
- small mixing bowl
- whisk
- large serving bowl
- jug

1

Add the green beans to a pan of boiling water for 2 minutes. Then add the broccoli and peas and simmer for 3 minutes, and then drain.

2

Make the dressing. Place all the ingredients in a bowl, season with salt and a little freshly ground black pepper and whisk until combined.

3

Place the salad leaves in a bowl and place the vegetables on top. Drizzle the dressing over the salad and toss together. Serve immediately.

Green salad

This salad makes a great accompaniment to grilled fish or chicken. You can add your own favourite vegetables – just remember to keep them green!

Tip

Once the vegetables are cooked, run them under cold water so they stop cooking and retain their colour.

Variation

There are lots of other
ingredients you can add to
couscous. Try including a
handful of nuts or some
cranberries. For a special
treat, add pieces of grilled
halloumi cheese.

Tomato and couscous salad

Salad makes a great light lunch or it can be eaten as an appetizer. This super salad is full of interesting ingredients and looks pretty on the plate. It's tasty, too!

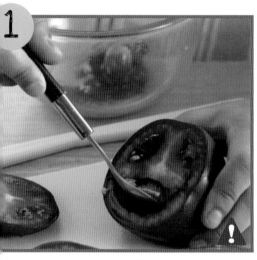

1

Slice the tops off the tomatoes and scoop out the insides. Put the seeds and flesh into a bowl with the tomato juice.

2

Pour the boiling water over the couscous, cover, and leave to stand for 10 minutes. Then, use a fork to fluff up the grains. Add the tomato mixture and stir.

3

Add the sultanas, basil, and parsley (if using), and mix. Taste, and season with ground black pepper as needed.

4

Spoon the mixture into the reserved tomato shells. Finally, serve with any leftover couscous mixture and garnish with some lettuce leaves.

30 mins   Serves 4

Ingredients

- 4 large tomatoes
- 150ml (5fl oz) tomato juice
- 125g (4½oz) couscous
- 150ml (5fl oz) boiling water
- 50g (1¾oz) sultanas
- handful of basil leaves, chopped
- handful of flat-leaf parsley, torn (optional)

Equipment

- sharp knife
- chopping board
- teaspoon
- small glass bowl
- large glass bowl
- fork
- tablespoon

Tuna and bean salad

30 mins   Serves 4

Ingredients

- 125g (4 ½ oz) frozen broad beans
- 400g can tuna in olive oil, drained
- 10 cherry tomatoes, halved
- handful of fresh chives, finely chopped
- ground black pepper
- 12 black olives, pitted
- 1 crisp lettuce such as Cos, leaves separated
- 2-3 spring onions, finely sliced

For the dressing

- 6tbsp extra virgin olive oil
- 1 garlic clove, finely chopped
- 2tbsp lemon juice
- 1-2tsp Dijon mustard

Equipment

- large glass bowl
- colander
- screw-top jar
- 4 serving bowls

Salads are good for you as they help you to get your five portions of fruit and vegetables a day. This salad is full of interesting ingredients and is fun to make.

1

Soak the broad beans in hot water for five minutes, then use a colander to drain. Set aside.

2

To make the dressing, put all the ingredients in a screw-top jar, season with black pepper, cover with the lid, and shake!

3

Put the tuna, tomatoes, and half of the dressing in a bowl. Sprinkle in half of the chives and season with the pepper. Gently mix in the beans and olives.

4

Spoon the tuna mixture on top of the lettuce. Drizzle with the remaining dressing, and sprinkle over the spring onions and remaining chives.

Variation

If you don't like tuna then you can swap it for 400g of cooked ham slices or cooked chicken pieces, shredded. Also, you can try green olives instead of black olives.

Rainbow salad

Food is full of colour, and this healthy salad with a tofu dressing will bring dynamic colour to the table. A serving bowl with blue in its pattern will complete the rainbow.

15 mins 10 mins Serves 4

Ingredients

- mixed salad leaves
- 2tbsp extra virgin olive oil
- 1tbsp mustard seeds
- 250g (9oz) fresh peas
- ½ yellow, ½ orange peppers, cut in strips

- 12 cherry tomatoes, halved
- 2 carrots,
- 2 raw beetroot, cut in strips
- 8 baby corn, cut in half lengthwise
- 1tbsp sesame seeds
- 2tbsp pumpkin seeds

Dressing

- 125g (5oz) silken tofu
- 2tsp sesame oil

- ½tbsp rice vinegar
- 1tbsp soy sauce
- 1tbsp extra virgin olive oil
- 1tbsp runny honey
- 1tbsp water
- mint, chopped
- salt and freshly ground black pepper

Croutons

- 6 slices wholemeal bread
- 2tbsp extra virgin olive oil

Equipment

- biscuit cutters
- baking tray
- pastry brush
- electric blender
- colander
- colourful serving bowl
- sharp knife
- large frying pan

1

Cut shapes out of the bread, using cutters. Brush the bread with olive oil and bake in the oven for about 5 minutes until golden brown.

2

Place all the ingredients for the dressing in a blender. Blend until smooth. Season with salt and pepper according to your taste.

3

Put the mixed leaves in a colander and wash. Drain well. Make a large bed of the leaves in a colourful serving bowl.

4

5

Scatter the pepper strips, fresh peas, and tomato halves on top of the salad leaves.

Heat the olive oil in a large frying pan and add the mustard seeds. Once they start to pop add the beetroot, carrot, and baby corn. Cook them until just tender then tip over the salad ingredients in the serving bowl. Drizzle the dressing over the salad.

Salad niçoise

Ingredients

- 3 eggs
- 225g (8oz) small new potatoes, washed
- 115g (4oz) French beans, trimmed
- 6 small tomatoes, quartered
- 2 x 200g (7oz) can tuna in olive oil, drained
- handful of fresh flat-leaf parsley, chopped
- bunch of fresh chives, finely chopped
- 12 black olives, pitted
- 50g (1¾oz) can anchovy fillets, drained
- 1 crisp lettuce, leaves separated and washed

For the dressing

- 6tbsp olive oil
- 2tbsp white wine vinegar
- 1 garlic clove, halved
- 2tsp Dijon mustard
- salt and freshly ground black
- pepper

Equipment

- saucepan
- colander
- knife
- serving bowl
- screw-top jar

This is a great salad if you want something that's quick to make, filling, and really tasty. A speciality of the Côte d'Azur region of France, and named after the city of Nice, Salad Niçoise is full of flavour, with salty anchovies and olives, juicy tuna, and fresh herbs.

1

Cook the eggs in a pan of simmering water for about 10 minutes. Cool in cold water and then remove the shells.

2

Boil the potatoes for about 10–15 minutes, or until tender when pierced with a knife. Drain and leave to cool, then cut in half, lengthways. Simmer the French beans in a pan of water for 3 minutes, then drain and cool in cold water.

3

Put the potatoes, beans, tomatoes, tuna, herbs, olives, anchovies, and lettuce leaves in a large serving bowl.

4

Put all the dressing ingredients in a screw-top jar. Season well with salt and freshly ground black pepper. Make sure the lid is on tight, then shake well to mix everything up.

5

Remove the garlic from the dressing, then drizzle it over the salad and gently toss together. Quarter the eggs and arrange them on top. Serve with lots of fresh crusty bread to mop up the juices.

Variation

Try slices of Greek halloumi cheese cooked on a hot griddle pan for 3 minutes on each side, or until it turns golden brown. Or use fresh mozzarella, torn into chunks, with a handful of fresh basil leaves.

Classic salads

These salads taste fantastic and healthy. Best of all, it won't take you long to prepare them. Try and use really fresh ingredients, which will have more flavour.

1

Mozzarella, avocado, and tomato salad

Mozzarella, avocado, and tomato salad tastes delicious with fresh ciabatta bread.

Ingredients

This recipe is for 4 people. It takes 10 minutes to prepare.

- 6 tomatoes, sliced
- 2 peeled avocados
- 3 125g (4¹/₂oz) balls buffalo mozzarella
- fresh basil leaves

Method

- Slice the tomatoes, avocados, and buffalo mozzarella balls and layer onto a plate.
- Scatter the fresh basil leaves over the salad, followed by a sprinkling of salt and plenty of freshly ground black pepper.
- To serve, drizzle some extra virgin olive oil all over.

2

Greek salad

This fresh and vibrant salad is great on its own with a chunk of bread, but also tastes wonderful as a side dish with grilled meats.

Ingredients

This recipe is for 4 people. It takes 15 minutes to prepare.

- 4 tomatoes
- ¹/₂ a sliced cucumber
- ¹/₂ a sliced red onion
- 1 sliced yellow pepper
- handful of black olives
- lettuce leaves
- 150g (5 oz) diced feta cheese
- oregano leaves
- 4tbsp olive oil
- fresh lemon juice

Method

- Chop the tomatoes into wedges and mix in a bowl with the sliced cucumber, red onion, yellow pepper, and a handful of black olives.
- Pile on top of some lettuce leaves, and top with the diced feta cheese and a few oregano leaves.
- Drizzle over the olive oil and a squeeze of fresh lemon juice.

Make your own

Feel free to make up your own salads, too – even a simple mix of crunchy green salad leaves is delicious with a tasty homemade dressing.

leaves

tomatoes

fresh herbs

olives

3

Potato salad

f you like hot and spicy flavours, try adding tbsp of horseradish sauce in step 2.

Ingredients

his recipe is for
people. It takes 10
inutes to prepare and
0 minutes to cook.

1¼kg (2¾lb) new
otatoes

4tbsp mayonnaise

2tbsp soured cream

2tbsp chopped fresh
hives

Method

● Cook the new potatoes in boiling water for 15–20 minutes,or until tender when pierced with a sharp knife. Drain and allow to cool.

● Mix the mayonnaise with the soured cream and fresh chives in a large bowl.

● When the potatoes are cool, cut them into bite-sized pieces. Stir into the mayonnaise mixture.

4

Coleslaw

This colourful recipe is great as a side dish. Try it on the side with sandwiches, burgers, or chicken. It's also great as a jacket potato topping!

Ingredients

This recipe is for
4 people. It takes
5 minutes to prepare
and 4 minutes to cook.

• 3tbsp plain yoghurt

• ½tbsp Dijon mustard

• 3tbsp mayonnaise

• ½ a white cabbage

• 2 large carrots

• ½ a sliced onion

• freshly ground black
pepper

Method

● To make the dressing, mix the plain yoghurt with the Dijon mustard and mayonnaise.

● Finely slice the white cabbage, grate the carrots, and mix with the sliced onion.

● Place all the vegetables into a large bowl, and stir through the dressing.

● Season to taste with freshly ground black pepper.

LIGHT BITES

Bruschetta

Bruschetta is a tasty Italian starter

or snack. It is traditionally made by piling ripe tomatoes onto toasted garlicky bread.

40 mins   5 mins   Serves 2

Ingredients

• 4 x 2.5cm (½in) slices Italian style bread, such as ciabatta

• 3 medium ripe tomatoes

• 1tbsp olive oil

• 6 basil leaves

• 1 clove garlic, peeled

Equipment

• knife

• chopping board

• metal spoon

• sieve

• bowl

• griddle pan

Halve and deseed the tomatoes. Press the seeds through a sieve over a bowl, then discard the seeds. Dice the tomatoes and add to the bowl.

Add the olive oil, salt and freshly ground black pepper. Leave to stand for 30 minutes. Roll up the basil leaves, chop finely, then add to the mixture.

Toast the bread on both sides, preferably in a griddle pan to create dark lines, or under a preheated grill.

Rub the warm bread with the clove of garlic. Place each piece of bread on a plate and heap with the tomato mixture.

Tip

Try adding some
torn mozzarella, which
can also be lightly
toasted under a grill.

Four ways with brushetta

Try out these these tasty bruschettas.

1

2

Tiny tomatoes

This is a delicious combination of ingredients and flavours. The mozzarella melts in your mouth and the tomatoes are so juicy.

Ingredients

This recipe is for 4 people. It takes 5 minutes to prepare and 2 minutes to cook.

• ciabatta loaf, sliced

• 125g (4½oz) mini mozzarella balls

• 1 punnet of tiny tomatoes

• 8 fresh basil leaves

Method

• Toast the slices of ciabatta until golden under a grill. You may have 1 or 2 slices left over at the end.

• Carefully slice the tiny tomatoes in half.

• Place the mozzarella balls and tiny tomatoes on the toasted slices of ciabatta.

• Scatter a couple of basil leaves on each slice of ciabatta.

• Serve as individual portions or on a large tray.

Criss-cross ham

The salty ham and melted cheese make this bruschetta a yummy starter. It will be a real winner with your friends or family.

Ingredients

This recipe is for 4 people. It takes 5 minutes to prepare and 4 minutes to cook.

• ciabatta loaf, sliced

• 125g (4½oz) ham

• 170g (6oz) Cheddar cheese

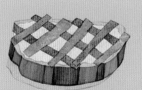

Method

• Toast the slices of ciabatta until golden under a grill. You may have 1 or 2 slices left over at the end.

• Cut the ham into thin strips and the cheese into generous slices.

• Place the cheese slices onto the ciabatta and then add the ham in a criss-cross pattern.

• Grill the bruschettas for 2 minutes or until the cheese begins to bubble. Be careful not to let the ham get overcooked.

• Serve as individual portions or on a large tray.

Make your own

Bruschetta is an Italian starter that traditionally consists of toasted bread with garlic, olive oil, salt and pepper. You can also try out these ingredients.

cheese

baby spinach leaves

red pepper

basil

roasted vegtables

salami

tomatoes

3

Carrot butter

The moist carrots and rich butter make this bruschetta a real favourite. You can keep any leftover mixture in the fridge for a few days.

Ingredients

This recipe is for 4 people. It takes 1 hour to prepare and ? minutes to cook.

1 ciabatta loaf, sliced

1 onion, finely chopped

4 carrots, finely grated

1tsp tomato puree

1tsp dried oregano

225g (8oz) butter

Method

• On a medium heat, fry the onions in a teaspoon of oil.

• Blend the onion, carrots, tomato puree, oregano and butter in a food processor.

• Place the mixture in a bowl, cover, and refrigerate the mixture for 1 hour.

• Toast the slices of ciabatta until golden under a grill. You may have 1 or 2 slices left over.

• Generously spread the carrot butter onto the slices of toasted ciabatta and serve as individual portions or on a large platter.

• Garnish with fresh coriander leaves if desired.

4

Cheese and cucumber

These bright and fun bruschettas are great for a party. Use the remaining cucumber to make sticks to accompany the dish.

Ingredients

This recipe is for 4 people. It takes 5 minutes to prepare and 4 minutes to cook.

• ciabatta loaf, sliced

• 200g (7oz) cream cheese

• 1 cucumber

Method

• Toast the slices of ciabatta until golden under a grill. You may have 1 or 2 slices left over at the end.

• Spread the cheese evenly over the bruschettas.

• Use a knife carefully to peel a cucumber and use cookie cutters to make decorative shapes out of the peel and flesh of the cucumber.

• Place the shapes on the bruschettas and serve on individual plates or on a large platter.

Filo and spinach tarts

The soft and creamy filling contrasts with the light crispy layers of filo pastry in this mouthwatering recipe for cheese and spinach tarts.

15 mins   25 mins   Serves 4

Ingredients

- 1tbsp sunflower oil

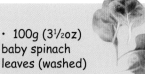

- 100g (3½oz) baby spinach leaves (washed)
- 125g (4oz) soft cream cheese
- 25g (1oz) Cheddar or Parmesan cheese (grated)
- 1 medium egg (beaten)
- Salt and freshly ground black pepper
- 16 x 12.5cm (5in) squares filo pastry

Equipment

- pastry brush
- 6-hole muffin tin
- chopping board
- sharp knife
- large mixing bowl
- wooden spoon
- dessert spoon
- oven gloves

Preheat the oven to 180°C (350°F/Gas 4). Use a pastry brush to apply oil to 4 muffin tin holes. Place the spinach on a chopping board and chop roughly, using a sharp knife.

Place the cream cheese in a bowl and beat with a wooden spoon until smooth. Then beat in the grated cheese and egg until combined. Season well, then stir in the spinach.

Brush one of the pastry squares with oil. Place another square over the top at an angle to make a star shape. Repeat with 2 more squares of pastry, brushing each with oil.

Gently press the layers of filo pastry into one of the holes of the muffin tin, and shape it to fit the hole. Repeat with the remaining pastry until you have 4 tarts.

Use a dessert spoon to fill each pastry case with the spinach mixture. Press it down with the spoon. Bake for 25 minutes until the pastry has browned and the filling has set.

Remove the tarts from the oven and allow them to cool in the tin for a few minutes, then carefully remove them from the tin. Serve hot with salad or vegetables.

Rice balls

This is a fun and easy snack to make. It also works well as a starter for a main meal. The soft rice and melted mozzarella are yummy and have a great texture.

30 mins 5 mins Serves 4

Ingredients
- 225g (8oz) cold cooked Arborio or other risotto rice
- ground black pepper
- 1 ball of buffalo mozzarella, cut into cubes
- 1 egg, beaten
- 2 slices of toast, for breadcrumbs
- olive oil, for deep frying
- salsa dip, to serve
- salad, to serve

Equipment
- mixing bowl
- large plate
- large dish
- small bowl
- sieve
- kitchen paper

Generously season the cold, cooked rice with black pepper. Roll the rice into 12 even-sized balls.

Push a cube of cheese into the centre of each ball, then cover so that the cheese is enclosed.

Roll each ball in the egg and then roll in the breadcrumbs (toast that's been turned into crumbs in a food processor).

Ask an adult to deep fry the balls in olive oil over a medium heat for 2 to 3 minutes or until golden.

Variation

Buy a salsa dip to serve the balls with. You can make this into a light meal by adding vegetables. Try a fresh garden salad with leaves, cherry tomatoes, and cucumber slices.

20 mins 5 mins Serves 2

Ingredients
- 2 red peppers
- 150g (5½oz) tinned chickpeas
- 1tsp paprika
- 1 clove garlic, peeled
- juice of ½ lemon
- 1tbsp tahini
- 3tbsp olive oil
- salt and pepper
- pepper shells, to serve

Equipment
- sharp knife
- chopping board
- baking tray
- silver foil
- plastic bag
- food processor
- desert spoon

Pepper houmous

Adding peppers to houmous gives a great zingy flavour. Make the presentation special and use any spare peppers as delicious little serving dishes. Add a little chilli if you like it spicy!

Cut each pepper into 4 and remove the stalks and seeds. Preheat the grill to high.

Line a grill tray with foil and place the peppers skin side up. Grill for 5 minutes or until the skins have blackened

Put the hot peppers into a plastic bag and seal it up. When the peppers are cool enough to handle, peel off the blackened skins.

Put the peppers, chickpeas, paprika, garlic, lemon juice, tahini, and olive oil in a food processor and blend until smooth. Season to taste.

Spoon the houmous into pepper shells and serve.

Tip

Serve the houmous with pitta bread and carrot and cucumber sticks. Don't forget to eat the pepper containers!

Shrimp skewers

Try out this filling and healthy dish. It's fun to create and tastes delicious. If you don't like fish you can use chicken instead.

25 mins. 15 mins Serves 4
plus chilling

Ingredients

- ½ a red pepper
- ½ yellow pepper
- 1 small courgette
- ½ red onion
- 8 cherry tomatoes
- 150g (5½ oz) cooked peeled king prawns
- salad to serve, optional

For the marinade

- juice of 1 lemon
- juice of 1 lime
- 2tbsp soy sauce (reduced salt)
- 1 garlic clove, crushed or finely chopped
- 1tsp light brown sugar

Equipment

- 4 kebab skewers
- rectangle dish that will fit the length of the skewers

Make the marinade by mixing the ingredients together in a jug. Carefully cut the peppers and red onions into chunks.

Chop the ends of the courgette off, then carefully slice the courgette into bite-sized chunks.

Thread the vegetables and prawns onto the skewers. Place the kebabs into a rectangle dish.

Pour the marinade over the kebabs. Put the kebabs into the fridge for an hour. Turn them over after 30 minutes.

Ask an adult to grill the kebabs for 15 minutes. Baste the prawns every 5 minutes with the marinade (discard any leftover marinade).

⏱ 40 mins, plus marinating   15 mins   🍽 Serves 4

Ingredients

- 12 skinless, boneless chicken thighs
- 1 red and 1 yellow pepper, deseeded and cut into chunks

Barbecue Sauce

- 6tbsp tomato ketchup
- 2tbsp maple syrup or clear honey
- 2tbsp dark soy sauce
- grated rind and juice 1 lime
- 2tsp freshly grated ginger
- 2tbsp soft brown sugar

Equipment

- small saucepan
- wooden spoon
- chopping board
- knife
- mixing bowl
- small wooden skewers (soaked in water for 30 minutes)
- pastry brush

1

Place all the ingredients for the sauce in a small pan, bring to the boil, then simmer for 2 minutes, stirring until the sugar has dissolved. Allow to cool.

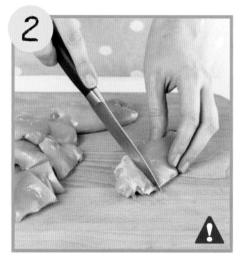

2

Cut each chicken thigh into 2 to 3 pieces. Place the cooled sauce in a large bowl. Turn the chopping board over.

3

Add the chicken, stir to coat, then leave to marinate for about 30 minutes.

4

Thread 2 to 3 pieces of chicken onto wooden skewers with pieces of red and yellow pepper. Repeat until all the chicken and peppers have been used up.

5

Line the base of a grill pan with foil, then grill for 10 to 12 minutes, turning occasionally and brushing with the sauce, until the chicken is thoroughly cooked.

BBQ chicken skewers

These bite-sized skewers are a tasty option. Make up double quantities of the sauce and use half for dipping if you like.

Tip

Remember to soak the wooden skewers in water for 30 minutes, to prevent them burning.

Four ways with Kebabs

Kebabs are fun and really easy to make

Chicken satay

This is a popular kebab recipe. Always soak the wooden skewers in cold water for 30 minutes to prevent them from burning.

Ingredients

This recipe is for 4 people. It takes 20 minutes to prepare and 16 minutes to cook.

· 500g (1lb 2oz) chicken breasts

· 1/2 lime, cut into wedges, to serve

Method

● Make up the satay sauce in a large bowl and set aside. Save a small amount to use as a dip.

● Cut up the chicken breasts into large chunks 4cm (1¹/₂in) cubes and place into the large bowl of satay sauce. Marinate in the fridge for 1 hour.

● Thread the chicken chunks onto short skewers (or large skewers cut in half). Discard any remaining marinade.

● Place the kebabs on a grill pan and cook for about 8 minutes. Turn over and cook for another 8 minutes. Serve the chicken warm with the satay sauce for dipping and wedges of lime.

> To make sure the chicken is fully cooked, pierce it with a fork to see if the juices run clear.

Ingredients

This recipe is for 4 people. It takes 80 minutes to prepare and 20 minutes to cook.

For the kebabs

· 250g (9oz) firm tofu

· 2 small courgettes, each cut into 8 wedges

· 2 medium red onions, each cut into 8 wedges

· 1 medium red pepper, deseeded and cut into 16 chunks

For the marinade

· 2 tbsp olive oil

· 1 tbsp soy sauce

· 3 tbsp black bean sauce

· 1 tbsp clear runny honey

· 2 garlic cloves, crushed

· salad, to serve

Tofu chunks

This colourful kebab would make a perfect vegetarian option for a summer barbecue.

Method

● Cut the tofu into 16 cubes. Put the cubes into a dish with the courgettes, onions, and red pepper.

● Mix the ingredients for the marinade in a large dish. Season. Use a spoon to coat the tofu and vegetables in the marinade. Put in the fridge for 1 hour.

● Thread the vegetables and tofu onto 8 skewers.

● Place the kebabs on the grill and brush them with the marinade. Grill for 15–20 minutes, turning them halfway through and brushing them with more marinade.

yellow courgette

mushrooms

onions

halloumi cheese

aubergine

Try your own

Play around with combinations of ingredients to make up your own kebabs. Use the barbecue sauce to create a beef and onion one. You can use the items pictured here, although not all on one kebab!

3

Lamb with mint

Lamb is delicious when flavoured with herbs and spices. You can make a mint and yoghurt dip to accompany this classic kebab.

Ingredients

This recipe is for 4 people. It takes 20 minutes to prepare and 20 minutes to cook.

- 450g (1lb) minced lamb
- 1 small onion, finely chopped
- 1 garlic clove
- 1/2 tsp ground cinnamon
- 2 tsp ground cumin
- 1 tsp ground coriander
- olive oil, for brushing
- 1 tsp dried mint
- 1/2 lemon, to serve

Method

● Put the lamb mince in a mixing bowl. Add the chopped onion, garlic, cinnamon, cumin, and coriander to the bowl. Stir the ingredients until they are all combined.

● Divide the lamb mixture into 12 pieces. Shape each one into a sausage and then thread them onto the skewers. Press or roll to lengthen the kebabs.

● Place the lamb kebabs onto the baking tray and brush them with oil. Grill them for about 5 minutes on each side, until golden. Transfer to a serving dish and sprinkle with mint.

4

Ingredients

This recipe is for 4 people. It takes 25 minutes to prepare and 15 minutes to cook.

For the marinade

- juice of 1 lemon
- juice of 1 lime
- 2 tbsp soy sauce
- 1 garlic clove, crushed
- 1 tsp light brown sugar

For the kebabs

- 1/2 red pepper
- 1/2 yellow pepper
- 8 cherry tomatoes
- 4 baby sweetcorn
- 150g (5 1/2 oz) cooked prawns

Prawn and peppers

This bright and colourful kebab is full of flavour. Squeeze lime juice on them to serve.

Method

● Make the marinade by mixing the ingredients together in a jug. Carefully cut the peppers and baby sweetcorn into chunks.

● Thread the vegetables and prawns onto the skewers. Place the kebabs into a rectangular dish. Pour the marinade over the kebabs. Put the kebabs into the fridge for an hour. Turn them over after 30 minutes.

● Grill the kebabs for 15 minutes. Baste the prawns every five minutes with the marinade (discard any leftover marinade).

Courgette frittata

Ciao! This recipe is not just an ordinary omelette, but an Italian one filled with your home-grown vegetables. Buon appetito! (Have a good meal!)

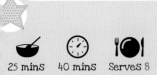

25 mins   40 mins   Serves 8

Ingredients

- 500g (18oz) new potatoes

- 50g (2oz) butter
- 1 large onion, finely chopped
- 3 courgettes, thinly sliced
- 1tbsp fresh mint leaves, chopped
- 8 eggs

- 75g (3oz) Pecorino cheese
- a pinch of ground black pepper

Equipment

- large saucepan
- colander

- knife
- chopping board
- large frying pan
- wooden spoon
- small bowl
- fork
- ladle

1

Cook the potatoes in boiling water for 15-20 minutes or until tender. Use a colander to drain them. Let them cool down, and then halve if large.

2

Melt the butter in a 28cm (11in) diameter, non-stick frying pan. Add the onion and cook gently until soft. Add the courgettes and cook. Stir often.

3

Stir in the potatoes and continue cooking for a further 5 minutes, until the courgettes have softened.

4

Crack the eggs into a bowl and add the Pecorino and mint and season well with pepper. Whisk together well using a fork.

5

Pour the egg mixture into the pan and turn the heat down as low as possible. Cook for 5 minutes until the eggs are just set.

6

Place the pan under a pre-heated grill for 5 minutes to brown the top. When ready, remove from the grill and leave the frittata to cool.

Ingredients

- 375g (12oz) ready-prepared puff pastry
- 250g (9oz) cherry tomatoes
- 250g (9oz) ricotta cheese
- 2 large eggs (beaten)
- 2tbsp freshly chopped basil
- 25g (1oz) Parmesan cheese (grated)
- Salt and black pepper

Equipment

- rolling pin
- baking sheet
- sharp serrated knife
- chopping board
- large mixing bowl
- wooden spoon
- oven gloves

Tomato and basil tart

This tart looks so impressive nobody will guess how simple it is to make! Serve it with salad and crusty bread for a delicious weekend lunch.

Preheat the oven to 200°C (400°F/Gas 6). Roll out the pastry, using a rolling pin on a lightly floured surface to a rectangle measuring about 25 x 38cm (10 x 15in).

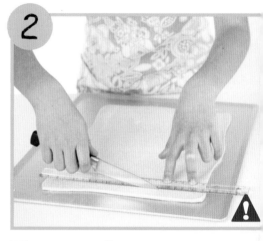

Place on a large flat baking sheet and using a sharp knife score a 2.5cm (1in) border along the sides of the rectangle, being careful not to cut all the way through.

Place the cherry tomatoes on a chopping board and use a sharp knife to cut the tomatoes in half. A knife with a serrated edge will make it easier to cut them.

In a large mixing bowl, beat together the ricotta cheese, eggs, basil and Parmesan cheese with a wooden spoon, until combined. Season with a little salt and freshly ground black pepper.

Spoon this mixture inside the marked edge and scatter over the tomatoes. Cook in the centre of the oven for 20 minutes until the pastry is risen and golden and the filling cooked.

20 mins   9 mins   Makes 24

Ingredients

- 400g (14oz) fresh salmon fillets
- 400g (14oz) cooked potato

- 50g (2oz) frozen peas, defrosted
- 150g (5½oz) fresh breadcrumbs
- 4tbsp freshly chopped parsley
- 2 eggs, beaten
- sunflower oil for frying

For the lemon mayonnaise

- 250ml (9floz) reduced fat mayonnaise
- grated zest and juice ½ lemon

Equipment

- medium saucepan or frying pan with lid
- 4 mixing bowls
- 3 metal spoons
- plate
- non-stick frying pan
- flipper

1

Place the fish in the pan. Add a little water, and bring to the boil. Cover and cook for 5 to 6 minutes. Allow to cool, then flake, removing any skin and bones.

2

Place the potato, peas and salmon in a bowl. Mix gently until combined and season to taste.

3

Mix the breadcrumbs with the parsley and place on a plate.

4

Place a heaped teaspoon of the salmon mixture in your hands, roll into a ball, then flatten. Dip into the egg, then coat in the breadcrumb mixture.

5

Heat a little oil in a frying pan and shallow fry the fish cakes for 2 to 3 minutes each side until golden.

6

Mix together the mayonnaise with the lemon zest and juice. Transfer to a bowl. Serve the fish cakes warm or cold on cocktail sticks with the dip.

Mini fishcakes

Serve these bite-sized fish cakes
on cocktail sticks to make them easier to dip
into the creamy lemon mayonnaise.

MAIN MEALS

Griddled chicken

Food has a wonderful texture and finish to it when it's been cooked in a griddle pan. Always make sure you cook the meat thoroughly. You can eat this dish hot or cold.

45 mins, plus chilling | 25 mins | Serves 4

Ingredients

- 2tsp paprika
- 5tbsp olive oil
- 4 skinless chicken breasts, each about 150g (5½oz)
- 400g (14oz) baby new potatoes, cut in half if necessary
- 2 spring onions, finely chopped
- 8 cherry tomatoes, halved
- 3tbsp chopped fresh mint
- 1tbsp lemon juice

Equipment

- large shallow dish
- tablespoon
- cling film
- griddle pan
- tongs
- small sharp knife
- chopping board
- medium saucepan
- colander
- large glass bowl

1

Mix the paprika and 3 tablespoons of olive oil in a large dish. Add the chicken and spoon over the marinade. Cover with cling film and chill for 30 minutes.

2

Heat a griddle pan until it is very hot. Reduce the heat to medium and place 2 chicken breasts in the pan. Griddle for 6 minutes on one side.

3

Carefully turn the chicken over using tongs. Spoon over a little of the marinade and then cook for 6 minutes, or until cooked through. Griddle the remaining chicken.

4

Put the potatoes in a medium saucepan and cover with water. Bring to the boil and cook the potatoes for 10 minutes or until they are tender.

5

Drain the potatoes and leave them to cool in a bowl. Add the mint. When cool, add the tomatoes and spring onions to the potatoes.

6

Mix the olive oil and lemon juice together, using a fork. Then pour the dressing over the salad and stir well to mix.

Four ways with roast vegetables

Each of these dishes can accompany a main meal.

1

Reds and greens

This vegetable medley is colourful and has a slight crunch. It could be paired with the Rice balls (pp78-79) or Griddled chicken (pp96-97).

Ingredients

This recipe is for 4 people when served as a side dish. It takes 8 minutes to prepare and 50–60 minutes to cook.

• 2 red onions

• 2 whole raw beetroots, peeled

• ½ head of broccoli

• 12 cherry tomatoes

• 1tbsp olive oil

Method

• Preheat the oven to 200°C (400°F/Gas 6).

• On a chopping board use a sharp knife to carefully cut the red onion into large chunks, slice the beetroot into large wedges, and cut the florets off the half head of broccoli.

• Place the beetroot into a roasting tin or oven-proof dish and use your hands to toss the vegetables with oil. Cook for 20 minutes.

• Add the remaining ingredients and cook for a further 30–40 minutes.

2

Sweet potato and parsnip

Perfect on a cold day, this option could be eaten with the hotpot recipes (pp138-140).

Ingredients

This recipe is for 4 people when served as a side dish. It takes 5 minutes to prepare and 50 minutes to cook.

• 4 large sweet potatoes, peeled

• 4 parsnips, peeled

• 1tbsp olive oil

Method

• Preheat the oven to 200°C (400°F/Gas 6).

• On a chopping board use a sharp knife to carefully cut the parsnips into large chunks and slice the sweet potatoes into large wedges.

• Put the parsnips and potatoes into a roasting tin or an oven-proof dish and use your hands to toss the vegetables with oil.

• Roast in the over for 50 minutes or until the vegetables are golden.

Try your own

There are plenty of other vegetables that taste delicious when roasted and work well as a side for any main dish. Try out these other ingredients.

tomatoes

mushrooms

butternut squash

leeks

olives

3

4

Pepper medley

Roasted garlic is really tasty and roasted peppers are juicy and full of flavour. This dish would sit well with chicken dishes.

Ingredients

This recipe is for people when served as a side dish. It takes minutes to prepare and 40 minutes to cook.

1 green pepper

1 yellow pepper

1 red pepper

1 orange pepper

1 garlic clove

2 small courgettes

1 tbsp olive oil

Method

● Preheat the oven to 200°C (400°F/Gas 6).

● On a chopping board use a sharp knife to slice the peppers into thin strips and the garlic in half.

● Carefully cut the courgette into thick slices.

● Place all the ingredients into a roasting tin or oven-proof and use your hands to toss the vegetables with oil.

● Cook for 40 minutes.

Roast potato and carrot

This is a classic choice of roasted vegetables that often gets served with chicken. It can help add carbohydrates to a lighter meal.

Ingredients

This recipe is for 4 people when served as a side dish. It takes 5 minutes to prepare and 50 minutes to cook.

• 12 Chantenay carrots, or 5 regular carrots

• 2 large potatoes, peeled

Method

● Preheat the oven to 200°C (400°F/Gas 6).

● On a chopping board use a sharp knife to quarter the potatoes and cut the carrots into thick wedges.

● Scatter the potatoes and carrots into a roasting tin or oven-proof dish and use your hands to toss the vegetables with oil.

● Cook for 50 minutes or until the vegetables are golden.

Lamb Kebabs

Ingredients

- 500g (1lb) lamb cut into 24 x 2.5cm (1in) cubes
- 1 green pepper (de-seeded and cubed)
- 1 red onion (halved)

For the marinade

- ¹/₂tsp of ground cumin
- ¹/₂tsp of dried oregano
- 1tsp of olive oil
- ¹/₂tsp of ground ginger
- 3 pinches of ground cinnamon
- juice of ¹/₂ orange
- 1tbsp of chopped fresh coriander (optional)
- 1tbsp of honey

For the couscous

- 1tbsp of olive oil
- juice of ¹/₂ orange
- ¹/₂ red onion, (finely diced)
- 175g (6oz) couscous
- 300ml (¹/₂ pt) stock
- 30g (1oz) sultanas
- 30g (1oz) blanched almonds (roughly chopped)
- 60g (2oz) dried apricots (quartered)

Equipment

- 2 mixing bowls
- dessert spoon
- cling film
- chopping board
- sharp knife
- 8 wooden skewers
- oven gloves
- grill and foil-lined tray
- tongs
- fork

This marinade adds a gentle spicy flavour to the lamb while the couscous is very simple to cook and is a great alternative to rice.

Mix all of the marinade ingredients together in a bowl. Stir in the lamb and cover with cling film. Leave to marinate for 1–2 hours in the fridge.

Cut each onion half into 4 equal wedges and remove the white core from each piece. Split the wedges in half to make 16 thin pieces of onion.

Place a cube of lamb onto a skewer, followed by pieces of onion and pepper. Repeat and add a piece of lamb to finish. Do the same for all 8 skewers.

Preheat the grill to a medium heat. Grill the kebabs for 12–16 minutes, turning every 2–3 minutes. Allow to rest before serving.

5

Meanwhile, pour the hot stock over the cous cous and mix them together. Cover the bowl with ling film until all the liquid has een absorbed.

6

Fluff the cooked cous cous with a fork to separate the grains. Stir in the orange juice, onion, apricots, almonds, sultanas, and olive oil.

Variation

Chicken or pork are tasty alternatives to lamb. Vegetarians could add extra vegetables, such as courgettes, mushrooms, or aubergines.

⬤ 20 mins 🕐 50 mins 🍴 Serves 6-8

Ingredients

- 350g (12oz) ready-prepared shortcrust pastry
- 150g (5oz) smoked or unsmoked streaky bacon

rashers (chopped)
- 3 medium eggs
- 150ml (¼pt) double cream
- 200ml (7floz) milk
- 1tbsp freshly chopped chives
- freshly ground black pepper
- 100g (3½oz) Gruyere cheese (grated)

Equipment

- rolling pin
- 23cm (9in) loose-bottomed quiche tin
- fork
- oven gloves
- baking paper

- baking beans or aluminium foil
- wooden spoon
- kitchen paper
- non-stick frying pan
- kitchen paper
- large mixing bowl
- balloon whisk
- baking tray

Preheat the oven to 190°C (375°F,/Gas 5). Using a rolling pin, roll out the pastry on a lightly floured surface. Line the loose-bottomed quiche tin with the pastry. Chill for 15 minutes.

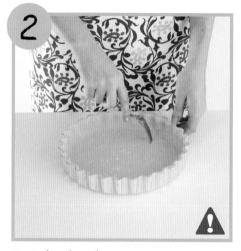

Prick the base with a fork, line with baking paper and fill with baking beans or scrunched aluminium foil. Bake for 15 minutes. Remove the paper and beans and bake for another 5 minutes.

Meanwhile, place the bacon in a non-stick frying pan and cook over a medium heat stirring occasionally until it is crisp. Drain the bacon on kitchen paper.

In a large mixing bowl, whisk together the eggs, cream, milk, chives, and freshly ground black pepper with a balloon whisk until they are thoroughly combined.

Place the pastry case on a baking tray. Scatter the cooked bacon and half the cheese over the pastry base. Pour over the egg mixture, then sprinkle it with the remaining cheese.

Place the tray in the oven and bake in the centre for 25–30 minutes until golden and set. Allow to cool for 5 minutes before serving in slices with salad.

Bacon and egg tart

When cooked, the cheese in this bacon and egg tart melts to form a lovely crispy top. Delicious hot or cold, the tart tastes especially good with salad.

Vegetarian moussaka

Traditional moussaka is made with meat and aubergine, but this vegetarian version is just as good! The pine nuts and cannellini beans give it a brilliant texture.

1

Preheat the oven to 200°C (400°F/Gas 6). Heat the oil in a pan over a low heat. Add the onion and sweat gently until soft. Stir in the mint and one teaspoon of the oregano.

2

Add the cannellini beans, passata, and pine nuts, and bring to the boil. Reduce the heat and simmer gently until thickened.

3

Spoon the bean mixture into an ovenproof dish. In a new bowl, mix together the yoghurt, egg, and remaining oregano. Spoon the yoghurt evenly over the top of the bean mixture. Bake in the oven for 15–20 minutes, until the top is golden and set.

15 mins   30 mins   Serves 4-6

Ingredients

- 1 tbsp olive oil
- 1 onion, finely chopped
- 1 tsp dried mint
- 3 tsp dried oregano
- 400g can cannellini beans, drained and rinsed
- 700g jar passata or 2 x 400g can of chopped tomatoes
- 100g (3½oz) pine nuts
- 250ml (8fl oz) Greek-style yoghurt
- 1 egg
- salad, to serve

Equipment

- frying pan
- wooden spoon
- ovenproof dish
- large spoon

Marinated chicken

The chicken in this recipe is marinated so that it absorbs the curry flavour. If you don't have time you can miss out the marinating and go straight to cooking in step 3. Alternatively, you could marinate for longer for a more intense flavour.

20 mins, plus marinating | 10 mins | Serves 2-4

Ingredients

- 2 chicken breasts (skinless and boneless)
- 125g (4oz) natural yoghurt
- 1tbsp of curry powder
- 2tbsp of vegetable oil
- juice of ½ lemon
- 1tsp of tomato purée
- salt and pepper
- 2tbsp of mango chutney (optional)
- 30g (1oz) sultanas (optional)
- 30g (1oz) flaked almonds (optional)

To Serve

- naan bread
- 1-2 Little Gem lettuces

Equipment

- mixing bowl
- dessert spoon
- 2 chopping boards
- 2 sharp knives
- frying pan
- wooden spatula

1

In a bowl, mix the tomato purée, oil, and curry powder together to make a paste. Add the lemon juice and half the yoghurt to make the marinade.

2

Carefully cut each chicken breast into cubes of about 2.5cm (1in). Turn the chopping board over.

3

Stir the chicken into the marinade, season with salt and pepper, and cover the bowl. Leave the chicken to marinate in the fridge for 30 minutes.

4

Place the frying pan over a medium to high heat and fry the chicken for 3–4 minutes. The chicken will change colour but it will not be cooked yet.

5

dd the sultanas and
lmonds and cook for 3–4 minutes.
efore serving, cut a piece of
hicken in half. If there is no
ace of pink, it is cooked.

6

To shred the lettuce, roll
up the leaves and carefully cut
them into thin slices. Serve the
chicken with the shredded lettuce
and naan bread.

Tip

Serve the yoghurt left over
from step 1 as a side dish.
The plain yoghurt tastes great
with the curry flavour of the
chicken. Stir in the mango
chutney for a fruity twist.

Potato fishcakes

Potatoes can be cooked in many ways; mashed, boiled, roasted, and baked. Bite into these crunchy fishcakes and the creamy fish and mash will melt in your mouth.

15 mins 25 mins Serves 4

Ingredients

- 250g (9oz) undyed smoked haddock, trimmed
- 1 fresh bay leaf
- 300ml (10fl oz) milk
- 375g (³/₄lb) potatoes, unpeeled, boiled, and mashed
- 8 spring onions, finely chopped
- 100g (3¹/₂oz) tinned sweetcorn
- 4 eggs, hard-boiled, peeled and chopped
- 2tbsp fresh parsley, chopped
- zest of 1 lemon
- 8tbsp double cream
- 2 egg yolks

- 2 eggs
- 100g (3¹/₂oz) flour
- 125g (4¹/₂oz) breadcrumbs
- 1tbsp butter
- 2tbsp olive oil
- salsa, to serve
- lemon wedges, to serve

Equipment

- shallow pan
- large mixing bowl
- fork
- spoon
- 2 small glass bowls
- whisk
- chopping board
- large shallow bowl
- large plate
- frying pan
- spatula

1

ook the haddock fillets with
e bay leaf and the milk in a shallow
n. Simmer for 5–10 minutes. Cool,
move the fish's skin and any bones,
d flake into chunks.

2

Mix the fish, potato, spring
onions, sweetcorn, chopped eggs,
parsley, and zest. In a small bowl,
beat the cream with the egg yolks,
and stir into the mixture.

3

Divide the mixture into
4 parts. Shape each part into
a slightly flattened ball. Roll each
fishcake in the flour on a plate.
Shaking off any excess.

4

rack two eggs into a small
wl and whisk. Transfer to a large
allow bowl. Dip each fishcake
to the eggs so that they get egg
l over the surface.

5

Dip egg-coated fishcake into
the breadcrumbs and coat all over,
then set aside. Repeat dipping into
egg then breadcrumbs with the
remaining fishcakes.

6

Heat the oil and butter in a
frying pan and add the fishcakes
carefully. Cook them gently for
about 4–5 minutes on each
side, or until golden brown.

Tomato and aubergine layers

Slow roasted tomatoes are chewy, juicy, and tasty. Everyone who tries this dish will love the combination of textures and flavours.

40 mins | 3 hrs 15 mins | Serves 4

Ingredients

- 6 large ripe tomatoes, cut in half
- 2 garlic cloves, finely chopped
- 1tbsp dried oregano
- 8tbsp extra-virgin olive oil
- 1 large aubergine, thinly sliced
- pinch of smoked paprika
- 8tbsp natural yoghurt
- 2tbsp runny honey
- 4tbsp sliced almonds, toasted

Equipment

- baking tray
- spoon
- colander
- large bowl
- griddle pan
- 4 serving dishes

1

Lay the tomatoes cut-side up on the tray. In a small bowl, mix the garlic and oregano, half of the olive oil, and season with salt and pepper. Spoon it over the tomatoes.

2

Preheat the oven to (150°C/ 300°F/Gas 2). Bake the tomatoes for 2–3 hours. When ready, they should be slightly shrunk, but still a brilliant red colour. Allow to coo

3

Layer the slices of aubergine in a colander, sprinkling a little salt between each layer. Leave for 30 minutes then rinse well with water and dry.

4

Place the aubergine slices in a large bowl, pour over the rest of the olive oil, and sprinkle with a little paprika. Toss together with your hands.

5 **Heat a ridged** griddle pan, then add a single layer of the aubergine slices. Cook each side until tender. Place the slices on a plate. Repeat for the other slices.

6 **To serve, layer** the tomatoes and aubergines in 4 dishes. Drizzle two tablespoons of yoghurt and half a tbsp of honey over each dish. Sprinkle half a tablespoon of almonds over each portion.

Beef pasta

5 mins   10 mins   Serves 4

This pasta dish is an easy main meal to make for you and your family. The combination of beef and mushrooms is super-tasty.

Ingredients

- 1 small onion, finely chopped
- $1/2$ tbsp olive oil
- ground black pepper
- 250g (9oz) good-quality beef mince
- 100g ($3^1/2$oz) mushrooms, finely chopped
- pinch of dried oregano
- 1 garlic clove, finely chopped
- 400g can of chopped tomatoes
- 1tbsp tomato puree
- 1tsp green pesto
- 200g (7oz) tortiglioni pasta

Equipment

- frying pan
- wooden spoon
- saucepan
- colander

Cook the onion in the oil over a low heat. Season with pepper, then stir in the beef and cook, stirring, until no longer pink.

Add the mushrooms, oregano, garlic, tomatoes, and tomato puree and stir well. Simmer for 10 minutes, then stir in the pesto.

Cook the pasta in a saucepan of boiling water according to the packet's instructions.. Using a colander, drain the pasta (over a bowl or sink), toss with the meat sauce, and serve.

Fresh tomato pasta

You don't need to cook the sauce for this pasta dish. It's deliciously fresh and fast to make. The classic flavours of tomato and basil are perfect together.

mins   10 mins   Serves 4

Ingredients

• 5 tomatoes, deseeded and roughly chopped

• 2 garlic cloves, finely chopped

• handful of basil leaves, torn

• 2tbsp extra virgin olive oil

• ground black pepper

• 200g (7oz) farfalle pasta

• Parmesan cheese, freshly grated, to serve

Equipment

• large glass bowl

• wooden spoon

• large saucepan

• colander

1

Put the tomatoes, garlic, basil, and olive oil in a large bowl and season with black pepper. Stir the mixture together using a wooden spoon.

2

Cook the pasta in a saucepan of boiling water according to the packet's instructions. Using a colander, drain the pasta well, then toss with the tomato sauce and serve.

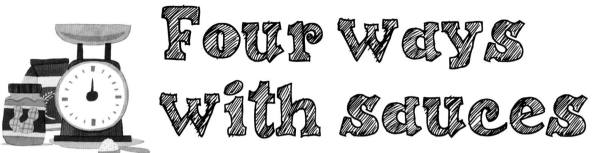

Four ways with sauces

Try these simple and versatile sauces.

(1)

Chunky tomato sauce

This sauce is hearty and full of flavour. It can be used in a lasagne if you double the quantities or as a simple sauce for a pasta dish.

Ingredients

This recipe is for 4 people. It takes 3 minutes to prepare and 5 minutes to cook.

- 1 onion
- 1 garlic clove
- 2tbsp olive oil
- 400g tinned tomatoes
- 1tbsp tomato puree

Method

• Chop the onion into small pieces and peel and crush the garlic clove.

• Pour the oil into a saucepan and add the onion and garlic. Fry gently for 2 minutes or until the onion is golden.

• Add the tinned tomatoes and puree to the saucepan, stir and cook for 3 minutes.

(2)

Crunchy satay sauce

You can use smooth peanut butter for this classic sauce, but crunchy peanut butter gives it a better texture.

Ingredients

This recipe is for 4 people. It takes 5 minutes to prepare and 6 minutes to cook.

- 1½ onions
- 3cm (1½ in) cube fresh ginger
- 3 garlic clove
- 4½tbsp vegetable oil
- 3tbsp soy sauce
- 9tbsp water
- 4½tbsp light brown sugar
- 15tbsp crunchy peanut butter
- juice of 2 limes

Method

• Peel the onion and chop it very finely.

• Peel the ginger and grate it coarsely, then peel and crush the garlic.

• Heat the oil in a saucepan. Cook the onion gently for 3 minutes or until soft. Add the ginger and garlic and cook fo a few minutes. Let the mixtur cool down.

• Put the onion mixture, soy sauce, water, sugar, peanut butter, and lime juice in a bowl and whisk.

Get these tools...

As the name suggests, a saucepan is for making sauces in. You will need these items in order to make most sauces. The wooden spoon is for stirring and the whisk is for blending the ingredients together.

saucepan

wooden spoon

whisk

knife

4

Cheesy white sauce

This sauce is often used in lasagne. You can also put it on pasta and add cooked bacon to make a cheesy, creamy pasta.

Ingredients

This recipe is for people (when used in a lasagne). It takes minutes to prepare and 6 minutes to cook.

- 0g (2oz) unsalted butter
- 30g (1oz) plain flour
- 500ml (16fl oz) warm milk
- 0g (2oz) Parmesan cheese, grated

Method

- Over a low heat, melt the butter in a small pan.
- Stir in the flour and cook for 1 minute. Gradually whisk in the milk. Stir and continue heating until thickened.
- Add in the cheese and season. Stir until the cheese is well mixed into the sauce.

Barbecue sauce

Tasty and sweet, this sauce uses the natural sugars from oranges and honey to give it a delicious flavour.

Ingredients

This recipe is for 6 people. It takes 10 minutes to prepare and works perfectly for a marinade.

- 2 garlic cloves
- 4tbsp tomato ketchup
- 4tbsp soy sauce
- 4tbsp fresh orange juice
- 2tbsp sunflower oil
- 6tbsp clear, runny honey
- 2tsp mustard

Method

- Crush the garlic cloves and put in a glass bowl.
- Add the ketchup, soy sauce, and orange juice to the bowl and mix well with a wooden spoon.
- Pour in the sunflower oil, runny honey, and mustard. Mix all the ingredients for 2 minutes or until everything has blended into a sauce.
- Use it as a marinade to flavour meat or vegetables.

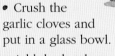

20 mins · 1 hr 15 mins · Serves 4

Ingredients

- 4 medium tomatoes, quartered
- 1 red onion, cut into 8 wedges
- 3 sweet potatoes, (about 450g (1lb)), peeled and thickly sliced
- 2 courgettes, sliced
- 1 red pepper, deseeded and cubed
- 1 yellow pepper, deseeded and cubed
- 500g (1lb 2oz) ricotta cheese
- 1tbsp olive oil
- 3tbsp freshly chopped basil
- 100g (3½oz) Cheddar cheese, grated
- 100ml (3½fl oz) double cream
- 1 medium egg, beaten
- 8 sheets fresh lasagne (about 125g (4oz))

Equipment

- chopping board
- knife
- 3 mixing bowls
- roasting tin
- metal spoon
- large ovenproof dish

1

Preheat the oven to 180°C (350°F/Gas 4). Place all the vegetables in a bowl and add the olive oil. Season with salt and freshly ground black pepper.

2

Place the vegetables in a roasting tin. Cook for 40 minutes, stirring occasionally until tender.

3

Meanwhile in a bowl, combine the ricotta with the cream, basil, half the cheese and the egg.

4

Arrange half the vegetables in the bottom of an ovenproof dish, place half the lasagne sheets over the top, then spoon over half the ricotta mixture.

5

Repeat once more, finishing with a layer of the cheese mixture. Sprinkle over the remaining cheese and bake for 35 to 40 minutes until golden and bubbling.

Sweet potato lasagne

This lasagne is lighter than a traditional lasagne. Ricotta cheese mixed with fresh basil replaces the traditional béchamel sauce.

Tip

Use fresh lasagne sheets as there is no sauce for dried sheets to soak up.

Chilli con carne

This dish has a kick to it so if you don't like your food too spicy then you should use less of the chilli. You can serve it with tortilla chips, salsa, and guacamole.

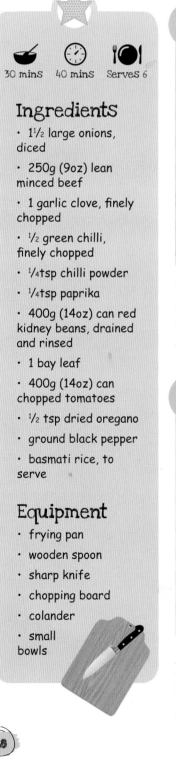

30 mins 40 mins Serves 6

Ingredients
- 1½ large onions, diced
- 250g (9oz) lean minced beef
- 1 garlic clove, finely chopped
- ½ green chilli, finely chopped
- ¼tsp chilli powder
- ¼tsp paprika
- 400g (14oz) can red kidney beans, drained and rinsed
- 1 bay leaf
- 400g (14oz) can chopped tomatoes
- ½ tsp dried oregano
- ground black pepper
- basmati rice, to serve

Equipment
- frying pan
- wooden spoon
- sharp knife
- chopping board
- colander
- small bowls

1

Cook the onions and meat for 5 minutes. Stir in the garlic, chilli, chilli powder, and paprika, and cook for 5 minutes.

2

Add the kidney beans and bay leaf, fry for 2 minutes.

3

Add the tomatoes and oregano. Bring to a boil, season with pepper, then simmer on a low heat for 40 minutes, stirring occasionally.

4

Cook the rice using the method on the packaging. Drain using a colander. Take the bay leaf out of the chilli.

Ask an adult
to cut up the chilli.
It can sting your eyes
if you accidentally
touch them.

Fish and wedges

Fish and chips is a favourite meal around the world. Try making sweet potato wedges instead of chips that normally accompany this dish.

30 mins   35 mins   Serves 4

Ingredients

- 125g (4½oz) plain flour
- 1tsp bicarbonate of soda
- 1tsp paprika
- 150ml (5fl oz) cold fizzy water
- Pinch of black pepper
- 250ml (8fl oz) sunflower oil
- 300g (10oz) white fish, such as pollock or haddock, cut into 1cm (½ in) strips

For the sweet potato wedges

- 2 large sweet potatoes
- 2tbsp olive oil

Equipment

- sharp knife
- large baking tray
- pastry brush
- large mixing bowl
- whisk
- deep-sided frying pan
- slotted spoon
- kitchen paper

1

Preheat the oven to 200°C (400°F/ Gas 6). Wash the sweet potatoes and carefully slice them into wedges.

2

Place the wedges in an large bakir tray and brush olive oil over them. Roas them for 25 minutes or until lightly browr

3

Put the flour, bicarbonate of soda, paprika, and fizzy water in a mixing bowl, season with black pepper, then whisk until smooth.

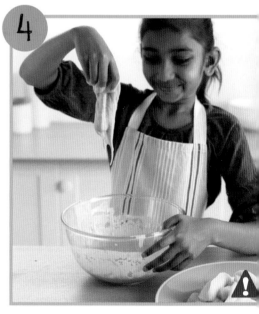

4

Ask an adult to heat the sunflower oil in a deep-sided frying pan. Coat the fish in the batter.

5

Ask an adult to cook the fish until it's golden brown. Remove the fish with a slotted spoon. Drain on kitchen paper.

121

Vegetable tart

1 hr 15 mins, plus chilling

1 hr 5 mins

Serves 4-6

Ingredients

- 225g (7¹/₂oz) plain flour + extra for rolling
- 1 pinch of salt
- 90g (3oz) unsalted butter (diced)
- 30g (1oz) vegetable fat or lard (cubed)
- 2tbsp of water
- 100g (3¹/₂oz) ham (cubed)
- 125g (4oz) sweetcorn
- 125g (4oz) peas
- 1 small leek (sautéed)
- 2 eggs (beaten)
- 100ml (3¹/₂ fl oz) milk
- 100ml (3¹/₂ fl oz) cream
- 30g (1oz) cheese (grated)

Equipment

- sieve
- mixing bowl
- fork
- tablespoon
- cling film
- rolling pin
- flan tin, loose-bottomed and fluted (approx. 20cm/8" in diameter)
- table knife
- greaseproof paper
- baking beans or dried kidney beans
- oven gloves
- jug
- whisk

This is a simple introduction to making savoury shortcrust pastry. Here's a top tip – when making savoury or sweet pastry, make sure that your hands are not too hot and the butter and water are also cool to give the pastry a lighter texture.

Sieve the flour and salt into a bowl. Using a fork, gently stir the diced butter and vegetable fat into the flour until they are completely coated.

Rub the butter and fat into the flour with your fingertips, until it looks like coarse breadcrumbs. Preheat the oven to 200°C (400°F/Gas 6).

Add the water, drop by drop, and stir it into the crumbs with a table knife. When the crumbs start to stick together in lumps, gather the pastry in your hands.

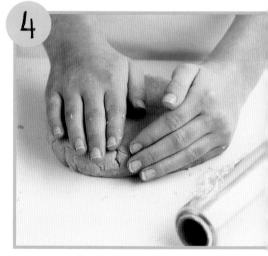

Shape the pastry into a smooth disc and wrap it in cling film. Chill it for 1 hour, or until firm. Lightly flour the work surface.

Roll out the pastry so
that it is slightly bigger than the
tin. Gently press it into the tin and
trim off the excess. Prick the base
and chill it for 15 minutes.

Add 2 layers of greaseproof
paper and the beans. Bake for 15
minutes, remove the paper and beans
and bake for 5 minutes. Reduce the
oven to 180°C (350°F/Gas 4).

Scatter the ham and vegetables
over the base. Whisk the eggs, milk,
and cream together and pour into the
tart. Sprinkle over the cheese and
bake for 45 minutes, before serving.

Mixed bean stir-fry

This vegetarian stir-fry is incredibly tasty and quick to cook. The dessicated coconut and cashew nuts give it a crunchy texture and delicious flavour.

30 mins, plus soaking | 10 mins | Serves 4

Ingredients

- 50g (1¾oz) dessicated coconut, unsweetened
- 2tbsp sunflower oil
- 1 garlic clove, sliced
- 6 spring onions, chopped
- 1 fennel bulb, sliced, core removed
- 500g (1lb 2oz) French and runner beans, thinly sliced
- 2tbsp soy sauce
- 1tbsp rice vinegar
- 100g (3½oz) beansprouts
- 1tbsp fresh coriander, chopped
- 200g (7oz) wholewheat noodles
- 1 tbsp sesame seeds
- 75g (2½oz) unsalted cashew nuts

1

lace the coconut in a bowl f warm water, cover, and leave r 20 minutes. Strain the coconut rough a sieve, pressing it against e sides.

2

Heat the oil in a large frying pan or wok. Add the garlic, onion, and fennel. Using a wooden spoon stir all the time for about 2 minutes.

3

Add your sliced beans and fry quickly, stirring all the time. Pour on the soy sauce and vinegar. Stir in, then remove the pan from the heat.

4

dd the beansprouts to e stir-fry. Sprinkle on the coconut nd coriander. Then give the ixture another good stir.

5

Cook some noodles following the instructions on the packet. Drain the noodles using a colander, then spoon them into your serving bowls.

6

Spoon out the stir-fry on top of the noodles. After roasting the cashew nuts and sesame seeds, sprinkle over and serve.

Rainbow beef

15 mins, plus marinating   10 mins   Serves 4

Ingredients

- 300g (10½oz) lean beef, cut into thin strips
- 1tbsp sunflower oil
- 1 red pepper, deseeded and cut into thin strips
- 6 baby corn, halved
- 75g (2½oz) mangetout
- 3 spring onions, sliced on the diagonal
- 2 cloves garlic, chopped
- 2tsp grated fresh ginger
- 4tbsp fresh orange juice

Marinade

- 6tbsp hoisin sauce
- 2tbsp soy sauce
- 1tbsp runny clear honey
- 1tsp sesame oil

Equipment

- small sharp knife
- chopping board
- spoon
- shallow dish
- wok or large frying pan
- spatula or wooden spoon
- tongs

Stir-frying is a quick and easy way to make a colourful and nutritious meal. You can serve it on its own or eat it with rice or noodles.

Put the marinade ingredients in a shallow dish. Mix them together and then add the beef strips. Coat them in the marinade, cover, and set aside for 1 hour.

Heat the sunflower oil in a wok or frying pan. Remove the beef from the marinade using tongs and carefully put it into the wok or frying pan.

Stirring continuously, fry the beef on a high heat for 1½ minutes or until browned all over. Remove the beef using the tongs and set aside.

Add a little more oil to the wok if it looks dry. Add the red pepper, baby corn, mangetout, and spring onions. Stir-fry for 2 minutes.

5 Add the garlic, ginger, beef, and leftover marinade and stir-fry for minute. Pour in the orange juice, and cook stirring, for another minute.

Variations
Strips of pork and chicken are a good alternative to the beef, or you could try prawns or tofu. For the best flavour, it's important to marinate them first.

Marinated lime chicken

The zingy lime and fresh coriander leaves give this dish a delicious combination of refreshing flavours. Serve with potatoes and your choice of vegetables.

15 mins, plus marinating   30 mins   Serves 4

Ingredients

- 4 skinless chicken breasts
- 2 eggs
- 175g (6oz) of breadcrumbs
- 4tbsp sunflower oil, for frying (1 tbsp per chicken breast)
- potatoes and beans, to serve

For the marinade

- juice of 4 limes, plus 1 lime finely sliced
- handful of coriander, finely chopped
- 2 garlic cloves, peeled and finely sliced

Equipment

- sharp knife
- chopping board
- mixing bowls
- large frying pan
- flipper

1 Carefully make 4 small cuts in the top of each chicken breast to help marinate flavour into the meat.

2 Make the marinade by mixing all the ingredients in a bowl. Place the chicken in the marinade. Cover the bowl with cling film and chill for one hour in a refrigerator.

3 Beat the eggs in a bowl and place one piece of chicken in the bowl. Turn the chicken breast so it gets covered in egg.

4 Coat the chicken breast in breadcrumbs. Repeat steps 3 and 4 for each piece of chicken. Discard any remaining marinade.

5 Fry the chicken in oil on a medium heat for 10-15 minutes on each side. Chicken needs to be cooked through with no sign of pink.

15 mins 40 mins Serves 4

Ingredients

- 25g (1oz) butter
- 25g (1oz) plain flour
- 300ml (½pt) chicken stock
- 100ml (3½fl oz) milk
- 2tbsp crème fraîche
- 1tsp dried mixed herbs
- salt and black pepper
- 1tbsp vegetable oil
- 1 small onion (sliced)
- 350g (12oz) chicken breast (cubed)
- 125g (4oz) cooked ham (cubed)
- 100g (3½oz) frozen peas
- 350g (12oz) ready-prepared puff pastry
- 1 egg (beaten)

Equipment

- medium saucepan with lid
- balloon whisk
- frying pan
- wooden spoon
- 4 individual pie dishes
- rolling pin
- sharp knife
- pastry brush
- oven gloves

Chicken and ham pies

These yummy pies have tender chicken and ham, cooked in a creamy sauce and topped with golden puff pastry.

Place the butter, flour, stock, and milk in a medium saucepan. Cook over a moderate heat, and continue whisking with the balloon whisk until the mixture starts to thicken.

Bring to the boil, then reduce the heat and add the crème fraîche and herbs. Season to taste with salt and freshly ground black pepper, then simmer for 2–3 minutes.

Heat the oil in a frying pan and add the chicken and onion. Cook for 3–4 minutes, stirring occasionally, until the onion has softened and the chicken has browned.

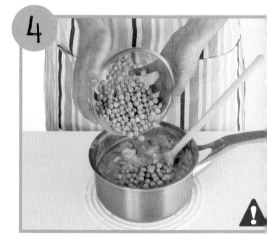

Stir the chicken and onions into the sauce, then cover and simmer for 10 minutes. Remove the pan from the heat and stir in the ham and peas.

5 **reheat the oven** to 200°C
00°F/Gas 6). Allow the mixture to
ool slightly, then divide it between
ur small individual pie dishes or
e large one.

6 **Roll out the pastry** on a
lightly floured surface, then cut
out four circles, slightly larger than
the top of the pie dishes. Use the
scraps to make thin strips to cover
the edges of the pie dishes.

7 **Brush the edges** of the pie
dishes with the egg, then press on
the strips of pastry. Brush with egg
again, then place the pastry lids on
top. Use your fingers to seal the
edges of pastry together.

8 **rush the tops** with egg
d make a cross in the top of
ch pie to allow the steam to
cape. Cook for 20 minutes at
e top of the oven, until the
stry is puffed and golden.

Variation

Use vegetable stock in step 1.
In steps 3 and 4, omit the
chicken and ham. Simmer the
sauce for 5 minutes and add
350g (12oz) cooked potatoes,
carrots and parsnip, and 75g
(3oz) sweetcorn when you
add the peas.

Vegetable lasagne

Ingredients

- 2 large red onions
- 2 large carrots
- 2 large courgettes
- 2 red peppers, de-seeded
- 1 medium aubergine
- 2 yellow peppers, de-seeded
- 4tbsp olive oil
- 2tsp chopped fresh rosemary
- 2 garlic cloves, crushed
- 400g can chopped tomatoes
- 1tbsp tomato puree
- 9 dried lasagne sheets

For the sauce

- 60g (2oz) unsalted butter
- 30g (1oz) plain flour
- 500ml (16fl oz) warm milk
- 125g (4½oz) Parmesan cheese, grated

Equipment

- chopping board
- sharp knife
- roasting tin
- oven gloves
- large saucepan
- wooden spoon
- small saucepan
- whisk
- lasagne dish (approx. 25 x 18cm and 5cm deep (10 x 7in and 2in deep)
- serving spoon

A crowd-pleasing dish that's a meal in its own right this lasagne makes a welcome change from the meat-based one. Why not experiment with other flavours?

Preheat the oven to 220°C (425°F/ Gas 7). Cut the onions into wedges and then chop all the other veg into chunks.

In the roasting tin, mix the oil, rosemary, and garlic with the vegetables and season. Roast for 35 minutes, shaking the tin occasionally.

Gently warm through the tomatoes and tomato puree in a large saucepan. Take the pan off the heat and carefully stir in the roasted vegetables.

On a low heat, melt the butter in a pan. Stir in the flour. Cook for 1 min. Whisk in the milk. Stir until thickened. Add half the cheese and season.

5

urn down the oven to
0°C (375°F/Gas 5). Spoon a third
the vegetables into the the dish
d top with 3 lasagne sheets.

6

dd another third of the
getables, top with another layer of
sagne, pour over half the sauce,
d then the remaining vegetables.

7

inally lay on the remaining
sagne sheets and drizzle over the
uce. Sprinkle the cheese over the
p and bake for 35 minutes or
til golden and bubbling.

Jambalaya

This lightly spiced Cajun rice dish originated in Louisiana in the USA. The recipe can be easily adapted by adding your favourite vegetables or tofu.

1

Heat the oil in a large pan. Add the chorizo and onion and cook for 2 to 3 minutes, until the paprika oil from the chorizo is released.

2

Add the chicken and cook for 3 to 4 minutes until lightly browned on all sides. Stir in the rice until coated in the oil.

3

Add the tomatoes, stock and herbs. Cover and simmer for 15 minutes, stirring occasionally.

4

Add the peppers, peas and spring onions and cook, covered for a further 10 minutes, until the rice is tender and most of the liquid has been absorbed.

5 mins   32 mins   Serves 4

Ingredients

- 1tsp sunflower oil
- 100g (3½oz) chorizo sausage, skin removed and chopped
- 1 onion, chopped
- 3 skinless chicken breasts, cubed
- 225g (8oz) easy cook long grain rice
- 400g (14oz) can chopped tomatoes
- 450ml (¾pt) hot chicken stock
- 1tsp dried mixed herbs
- 1 red and green pepper, de-seeded and cubed
- 50g (2oz) frozen peas
- 6 spring onions, chopped

Equipment

- large saucepan
- wooden spoon
- heatproof jug

15 mins   14 mins   Serves 4

Ingredients

- 1 clove garlic, crushed
- 2.5cm (1in) piece root ginger, peeled and grated
- 1tbsp light soy sauce
- 1tbsp rice wine vinegar or sherry
- 350g (12oz) beef steak, (e.g. rump) thinly sliced
- 225g (8oz) dried egg noodles
- 1tbsp sunflower oil
- 75g (3oz) mangetout, halved
- 100g (3½oz) small broccoli florets
- 3 spring onions, sliced
- 1 red pepper, deseeded and thinly sliced
- 100g (3½oz) beansprouts
- 2tbsp oyster sauce
- 2tsp toasted sesame oil

Equipment

- mixing bowl
- metal spoon
- saucepan
- wooden spoon
- wok/frying pan

1

In a bowl, mix together the garlic, ginger, soy sauce, and rice wine vinegar or sherry. Add the sliced beef and stir, then leave to marinate for 10 minutes.

2

Meanwhile, cook the egg noodles. Place in a pan of boiling water and cook for 4 minutes. Turn off the heat. Drain the noodles and return to the pan to keep warm.

3

Heat the sunflower oil in a large wok or frying pan. Add the beef and stir fry for 4 to 5 minutes until browned.

4

Add the mangetout, broccoli, spring onions, and pepper. Stir fry for 2 to 3 minutes.

5

Add the noodles, beansprouts, oyster sauce, and sesame oil, then stir fry for a further 2 minutes.

Beef chow mein

'Chow mein' means stir-fried noodles in Chinese Mandarin. You can add whatever you like. Try fish, meat, tofu, prawns or vegetables.

Tip

To be totally authentic, try using chopsticks to eat this oriental dish

Lamb hotpot

This hotpot is a hearty main meal that will fill you up. The lamb and tomatoes make it juicy and the chickpeas add texture. Serve it with crusty bread rolls.

Cut the lamb, flour, and paprika into a mixing bowl and combine well so that the lamb is coated.

Heat the oil in a large pan over a medium heat, add the onions, and cook, stirring often, for 5 minutes. Add the lamb and cook until browned.

Stir in the garlic and chickpeas, and cook for 1 minute. Add the tomatoes, bring to the boil, then simmer for 15 minutes.

Season well with ground black pepper, stir in the spinach, and cook for 3 minutes.

25 mins   20 mins   Serves 6-8

Ingredients

- 175g (6oz) lean lamb (leg or fillet), cut into 2cm (¾in) diced
- ½tbsp plain flour
- ¼tsp paprika
- 1½tbsp olive oil
- ½ large red onion, diced
- 1½ garlic cloves, chopped
- ½ 400g can chickpeas, drained and rinsed
- 400g (14oz) can chopped tomatoes
- ground black pepper
- 125g (4½oz) baby leaf spinach
- crusty bread rolls, to serve (optional)

Equipment

- mixing bowl
- large saucepan
- wooden spoon

⌣ 20 mins 　 🕐 45 mins 　 🍴 Serves 4

Ingredients

- 2 eating apples
- 2tbsp olive oil
- 6-8 sausages, turkey, pork, beef, or vegetarian
- 1 onion, chopped
- 1 carrot, diced
- 2 cloves garlic, finely chopped
- 110g (4oz) lean back bacon, cut into bite-sized pieces, optional
- 1tsp mixed herbs
- 400g (14oz) tinned borlotti or pinto beans, drained and rinsed
- 4tbsp tinned chopped tomatoes
- 1tbsp tomato puree
- salt and pepper
- 400ml (14fl oz) chicken or vegetable stock

Equipment

- vegetable peeler
- small sharp knife
- chopping board
- large ovenproof pan with lid or large saucepan and large casserole dish with lid
- oven gloves
- wooden spoon
- jug
- tongs

1

Carefully remove the skin of the apples using a vegetable peeler. Quarter them and remove the core. Cut the apples into bite-sized pieces and set aside.

2

Preheat the oven to 200°C (400°F/Gas 6). Heat the oil in a large saucepan or ovenproof pan and cook the sausages for 5 minutes, or until browned all over.

3

Remove the sausages from the pan and set aside. Put the onion and carrot into the pan and fry over a medium heat for 5 minutes, stirring frequently.

4

Next, add the garlic, bacon, and herbs, stir well, and cook for 6 minutes. (Transfer to a large casserole dish if you aren't using an ovenproof pan.)

5

Add the beans, tomatoes, tomato purée, apples, and sausages and stir. Pour in the stock and bring to the boil.

6

Cover with a lid and place in the preheated oven. Cook for 25 minutes. The sauce should reduce and thicken and the apples will become tender.

Sausage hotpot

Fruit gives this savoury dish a natural sweetness and an extra vitamin boost. You can serve this winter warmer with fluffy mash and steamed green vegetables.

7 **Take care** when removing the casserole dish from the oven as the hotpot will be very hot. Season with salt and pepper.

DESSERTS

Yoghurt ices

You can use your favourite flavours to make this alternative to ice cream. What a great way to cool down on a hot summer's day!

20 mins | 4 hrs (freezing) | Serves 4-6

Ingredients

- 150ml (¼pt) double cream
- 30g (1oz) icing sugar
- 500g (1lb) natural yoghurt
- 90g (3oz) chocolate cookies
- 90g (3oz) soft fudge
- 60g (2oz) mini marshmallows
- 60g (2oz) honeycomb (optional)

Equipment

- chopping board
- sharp knife
- mixing bowl
- sieve
- whisk
- spatula or metal spoon
- 2 plastic tubs with lids

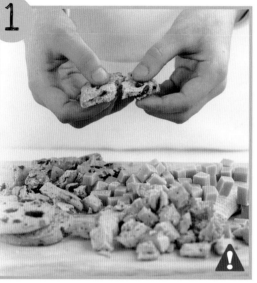

1

Carefully chop the fudge and honeycomb into tiny pieces and break the cookies into slightly larger pieces. Leave to one side.

2

Pour the cream into the mixing bowl and sieve in the icing sugar. Lightl whip the cream to soft peaks. (You cou use an electric or hand whisk.)

3

Gently fold the yoghurt honeycomb, fudge, cookies, and marshmallow pieces into the cream using a plastic spatula or metal spoon.

4

Spoon the mixture into the tubs, cover, and freeze. Stir the mixture after 2 hours to prevent ice crystals forming and then freeze for at least 2 more hours.

Variation

Try out this recipe with 300g (10oz) of your favourite ingredients, eg. bananas, strawberries, meringues, chocolate chips, or chopped up bars of chocolate.

Fruit pops

Make your own delicious frozen lollipops with this simple mix-and-match recipe. Create colourful combinations with layers of fruit, yoghurt, and pure juice. These lollipops are an excellent source of vitamins and they are a great way to cool down on a hot summer's day!

20 mins | 3-4 hrs (freezing) | Makes 6

Ingredients

- 300ml (½ pt) orange juice
- 300g (10oz) strawberries
- 3 large kiwi fruits
- 3tbsp of icing sugar

Equipment

- sharp knife
- chopping board
- food processor
- sieve
- wooden spoon
- 2 mixing bowls
- 6 lollipop moulds
- 6 lollipop sticks
- teaspoon

First, rinse and drain the strawberries in cold water. Then hull and quarter the strawberries and put them into a food processor.

Cut a thin slice off the top and bottom of each kiwi fruit. Working from top to bottom, carefully slice the skins off and then roughly chop the kiwis.

In a food processor, blend the strawberries with 1tbsp of the icing sugar. Sieve the strawberry purée into a bowl and throw away the seeds.

Wash the food processor and sieve – be careful of the blades. Blend the kiwi fruit with 2tbsp of icing sugar. Sieve the kiwi purée into a bowl and throw away the seeds.

dd the first layer and
eeze for 1 hour to set. Add the
ext layer and push the stick gently
to the first layer. Freeze for 1 hour
d add the last layer.

Do not fill the moulds right
to the top as the mixture will
expand a little as it freezes. Freeze
the lollipops for a final 1–2 hours
before eating.

Variation

Any of your favourite fruits or
fruit juices would taste great
in this recipe. Try stirring
100g (3½oz) strawberries into
300g (10oz) of flavoured
yoghurt to make 4
creamy lollipops.

Berry alternative

If blueberries aren't your favourite, then you can use blackberries or raspberries instead. Whichever you choose, the finished result will still be a knockout.

Blueberry cheesecake

These layered desserts look impressive but are easy-peasy to make. Making them in glasses means you can see the colourful layers.

Place three-quarters of the berries and half of the sugar into a small saucepan. Cover and simmer for minutes until soft. Stir in the other berries and leave to cool.

Using a clean wooden spoon, beat the cream cheese, crème fraîche, remaining sugar, and vanilla extract together in a mixing bowl. Continue until well mixed and soft.

Create a layered look by filling glasses with a spoonful of the blueberry sauce, then a spoonful of the cream cheese mixture, and then a spoonful of the crushed biscuits.

Repeat the layers once more and then put the filled glasses in the refrigerator for an hour to give the mixture time to set. Serve chilled straight from the fridge.

20 mins, plus setting time | 10 mins | Serves 4

Ingredients

- 500g (1lb 2oz) blueberries
- 2tbsp caster sugar
- 250g (9oz) cream cheese
- 200ml (7fl oz) crème fraîche
- 1/4tbsp vanilla extract
- 8 oat biscuits, crushed

Equipment

- small saucepan
- wooden spoon
- bowl
- dessert spoon
- 4 glasses

Apple crumble

In this twist on a classic dessert, apples are cooked in a rich butterscotch sauce, topped with a crunchy, buttery crumble. Serve with custard or ice cream for the ultimate pudding!

20 mins   40 mins   Serves 4-6

- 25g (1oz) butter
- Finely grated zest and juice ½ lemon
- ¼tsp salt
- 100ml (3½floz) water

- 75g (3oz) butter (diced)
- 25g (1oz) oats
- 50g (2oz) caster sugar

- sharp knife
- 900ml (2 pt) ovenproof dish
- medium saucepan
- wooden spoon
- large mixing bowl
- oven gloves

Ingredients
- 650g (1½lb) cooking apples
- 75g (3oz) light muscovado sugar

For the crumble
- 125g (4oz) plain flour

Equipment
- peeler
- chopping board
- corer

Preheat the oven to 180°C (350°F/Gas 4). Using a peeler, peel the apples to remove the skin. Place on a chopping board and use a corer to remove the apple cores.

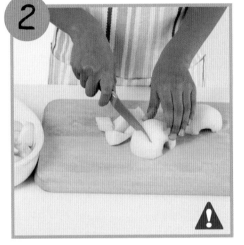

On the chopping board, cut the apples carefully into 2.5cm (1in) cube pieces with a sharp knife. Place the pieces in the bottom of an ovenproof dish.

Place the sugar, butter, lemon zest, and juice and salt in a saucepan with the water. Bring to the boil, stirring occasionally, until the sugar has dissolved and the butter has melted.

Pour the butterscotch mixture over the chopped apples in the ovenproof dish and stir with a wooden spoon until the apples are coated evenly in the sauce.

Place the flour in a mixing bowl with the diced butter. Using your fingertips, rub in the butter until the mixture looks like rough crumbs. Stir in the oats and the sugar.

Spoon the crumble mixture over the top of the apples and bake in the oven on the top shelf for 35–40 minutes until bubbling and golden. Allow to stand for 5 minutes before serving.

Fruit crumble

Crumble is a traditional English dessert and it tastes great served with cream, ice cream, or custard. Like all fruits, blackberries and peaches are a good source of vitamins, while the oats used in the crumble topping provide carbohydrates and fibre.

30 mins | 35 mins | Serves 4-6

Ingredients

- 4 large ripe peaches (or 6 small ones)
- 250g (8oz) ripe blackberries
- 60g (2oz) demerara sugar
- 3 pinches of ground cinnamon

For the crumble

- 125g (4oz) plain flour
- 125g (4oz) jumbo rolled oats
- 125g (4oz) demerara sugar
- 150g (5oz) unsalted butter (diced)

Equipment

- chopping board
- sharp knife
- teaspoon
- 2 mixing bowls
- metal mixing spoon
- sieve
- wooden spoon
- ovenproof dish (approx. 23 x 15cm and 5cm deep or 9 x 6in and 2in deep)
- baking tray
- oven gloves

1

Preheat the oven to 190°C (375°F/ Gas 5). Cut round the peaches and then twist them so that they split in half. Scoop the stones out with a teaspoon.

2

Slice the halved peaches in half again and then chop each piece into 3 more chunks. Rinse and thoroughly drain the blackberries.

3

Mix the sugar and cinnamon together in a bowl. Fold in the peaches and blackberries until they are completely coated in the sugar mixture.

4

Sieve the flour into a separate bowl and stir in the demerara sugar. Add the oats to the bowl and stir them into the flour and sugar.

sing your fingertips, rub
e diced butter into the flour mixture.
he mixture should come together
 small lumps when it is ready.

Place the dish on a baking tray
and spoon in the fruit filling. Scatter
the topping over and bake the crumble
for 30 minutes or until golden.

Variation

Other fruits such as
raspberries, apples,
plums, or blueberries
would taste great in
this recipe.

Apple pie

Ingredients

- 225g (7½oz) plain flour
- 1 pinch of salt
- 125g (4oz) unsalted butter (diced)
- 1 egg yolk (beaten with 1tbsp water)
- 2tbsp of caster sugar
- 1 egg beaten (for glazing)

For the filling

- 750g (1½lb) apples (peeled, cored, and cut into wedges)
- 1tsp of vanilla extract
- ½tsp of ground cinnamon
- 60g (2oz) soft light brown sugar
- ½ orange (zest and juice)
- 60g (2oz) chopped walnuts (optional)

Equipment

- sieve
- 2 large mixing bowls
- fork
- table knife
- cling film
- wooden spoon
- pie dish (approx 22cm /8½in in diameter)
- rolling pin
- pastry brush
- oven gloves

When making a sweet or savoury pie, make a hole in the top of the pastry, before you bake it. This allows the steam to escape and stops the pastry going soggy! Making sweet pastry is very similar to savoury pastry so read the recipe carefully to note the important differences!

1

Sieve the flour and salt into a bowl and stir in the sugar. Using a fork, gently stir the diced butter into the flour until it is completely coated.

2

Using your fingertips, rub the diced butter into the flour. When the butter is fully mixed in, the mixture will look like coarse breadcrumbs.

3

Stir the water and egg yolk (drop by drop) into the crumbs with a table knife until they stick together in lumps. Gather the pastry in your hands.

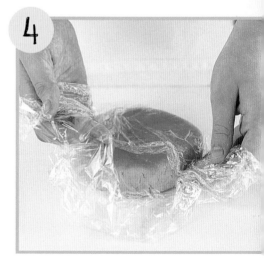

4

Put the pastry onto a lightly-floured work surface and shape it into a smooth disc. Wrap the disc in cling film and chill it for 1 hour, or until firm.

reheat the oven to 220°C
25°F/Gas 7). Mix the sugar,
nnamon, vanilla extract, orange
ice, zest, walnuts, and apples
gether in a bowl.

Tip the filling into the dish.
Dampen the edge of the dish. Roll
the pastry out to about 3mm (⅛in)
thick and place it over the dish.
Trim the excess.

Press the edges of the pastry
into the dish and crimp with a fork.
Glaze the pie with egg and make a
hole in the centre. Bake for 30–35
minutes, until golden.

Cherry and berry pie

This pie is really easy to make – you simply scrunch up ready-prepared puff pastry and fill with your favourite berry fruits! You can serve it with a scoop of vanilla ice cream or cream.

Ingredients

- 500g (1lb 2oz) ready-prepared puff pastry
- 1 egg (beaten)

- 2tbsp semolina
- 650g (1lb 6oz) mixed berries e.g. stoned cherries, blueberries, raspberries, red- and blackcurrants

- 2tbsp caster sugar
- icing sugar (for dusting)

Equipment

- rolling pin
- 30cm (12in) plate
- sharp knife

- baking sheet
- pastry brush
- teaspoon
- large mixing bowl
- large metal spoon
- oven gloves

1 Preheat the oven to 200°C (400°F/Gas 6). Roll out the pastry on a lightly floured surface. Cut around a 30cm (12in) plate with a sharp knife to make a circle.

2 Place the pastry circle on a baking sheet. Use a pastry brush to spread the beaten egg on the pastry, then sprinkle over 1tbsp of the semolina with a teaspoon.

3 In a large mixing bowl, place the mixed berries, remaining semolina, and 1tbsp caster sugar. Use a large metal spoon to gently mix together, taking care not to crush the berries.

4 Pile the fruit in the centre of the pastry, away from the edge. Scrunch up the edges of the pastry, bringing them towards the centre, but leaving the middle exposed.

5 Brush the scrunched pastry edges with more beaten egg and sprinkle the pastry with the remaining sugar. Chill for 30 minutes in the fridge.

6 Bake the pie at the top of the oven for 30 minutes until golden. If the pastry starts to become too brown, cover the pie with foil. Dust with icing sugar and serve in slices.

20 mins | 20 mins | Serves 8

Ingredients

- 250g (9oz) digestive biscuits
- 125g (4oz) butter

For the filling

- 125g (4oz) butter (diced)
- 125g (4oz) light soft brown sugar
- 400g (14oz) can sweetened condensed milk
- 150ml (¼pt) double cream
- 2 bananas (sliced)

To decorate

- grated milk chocolate or flaky chocolate bar and slices of banana

Equipment

- food processor or food bag and rolling pin
- non-stick saucepan
- wooden spoon
- 19cm (7½in) loose-bottomed fluted flan tin, 4cm (1½in) deep
- large mixing bowl
- electric or hand whisk
- spoon

1

Place the biscuits in a food processor and process until smooth. If you don't have a food processor, place the biscuits in a food bag and crush them with a rolling pin.

2

Melt the butter for the base in a saucepan, then stir in the crushed biscuits with a wooden spoon. Press the mixture into the base and sides of the tin. Chill the base for 30 minutes.

3

Place the diced butter an sugar in the saucepan over a low heat, and stir until the butter has melted. Add the condensed milk and gently bring to the boil, stirrin continuously.

4

Boil the butter, sugar, and condensed milk for 5 minutes, stirring continuously until it is a pale caramel colour. Pour over the biscuit base and chill for 1 hour.

5

In a large mixing bowl, whip the cream with an electric or hand whisk until it forms soft peaks. Arrange the banana slices over the toffee, then spoon over the whipped cream.

6

Decorate the top of the pie with extra sliced banana and som grated milk chocolate. Serve the pie in slices. Keep chilled and eat within 2 days.

Banoffee Pie

This divinely decadent caramel and banana
pie is definitely for those with a sweet tooth!

30 mins, plus chilling | 1 hour 30 mins | Makes 6

Ingredients

- 500g (18oz) pumpkin, cut into large chunks
- 1tbsp olive oil
- 375g (15oz) puff pastry, cut into 16 pieces
- 1tbsp plain flour
- 90g (3oz) treacle
- 1 whole egg
- 3 large egg yolks
- 300ml (11fl oz) milk
- ½ a split vanilla pod
- a pinch of salt

Equipment

- baking tray
- rolling pin
- bun tin
- parchment paper
- baking beans
- saucepan
- knife
- whisk
- mixing bowl
- sieve
- spoon

1

Preheat the oven to 190°C (370°F/Gas 5). On a baking tray, evenly coat them the pumpkin pieces with olive oil. Roast for 30 minutes until tender. Cool and then mash with a fork.

2

Shape the puff pastry pieces into balls. Roll out each ball until about 6cm (2½in) diameter. Press each piece into a bun tin, then chill in the fridge for 30 minutes.

3

Place a piece of parchment paper into each pastry and fill to the top with baking beans. Bake in the oven for 15 minutes then remove the paper and beans.

4

Pour the milk into a pan. Scrape out the vanilla seeds from the pod and add to the milk. Heat the mixture until just below boiling point. Leave to cool a little.

5

Lightly beat the egg yolks, whole egg, and treacle in a bowl. Add the flour and salt and beat until smooth. Strain the hot milk over the mixture and beat.

6

Pour the smooth mixture into a pan and bring to the boil, stirring all the time until thickened. Remove from heat and stir in the pumpkin puree.

Mini pumpkin pies

Ask an adult to cut the pumpkin in half with a sharp knife, using a rocking motion. Scoop out the seeds. Slice the pumpkin into pieces, and cut off the skin.

Spoon out the mixture evenly into the pastry cases. Bake in the oven for 20-25 minutes until just firm and slightly puffed up. Serve the pies warm with a dusting of icing sugar on the top if you wish.

Strawberry tartlets

These pretty tartlets taste as good as they look! Make them when the fruit is in season for the best flavour or frozen will also work.

20 mins   15 mins   Makes 8

Ingredients

- 225g (8oz) ready-prepared shortcrust pastry
- 150g (5oz) mascarpone cheese
- ½tsp vanilla extract
- 2tbsp icing sugar
- 175g (6oz) strawberries or other soft fruit
- 4tbsp redcurrant jelly
- 1tbsp water

Equipment

- rolling pin
- 9cm (3½in) fluted cutter
- 12-hole bun tin
- 8 pieces of aluminium foil
- oven gloves
- cooling rack
- small mixing bowl
- wooden spoon
- sieve
- chopping board
- sharp knife
- teaspoon
- small saucepan
- pastry brush

1

Preheat the oven to 200°C (400°F/Gas 6). Thinly roll out the pastry, then using a 9cm (3½in) fluted cutter, cut out 8 circles. Press the pastry circles into a bun tin.

2

Press a piece of scrunched-up foil into each case. Cook for 10 minutes, then remove the foil carefully. Return to the oven for 3–4 minutes. Cool in the tin, then transfer to a cooling rack.

3

To make the filling, place the mascarpone cheese and vanilla extract in a small mixing bowl. Sift over the icing sugar, then beat with a wooden spoon until smooth.

4

Place the strawberries on a chopping board. Remove the green stalk from the strawberries. Then use a sharp knife to cut them in half. (Quarter them if the strawberries are large.)

5

When the pastry cases

re completely cool, use a teaspoon
o fill them with the mascarpone
nd vanilla mixture. Arrange the
rawberries over the top.

6

Place the redcurrant jelly

in a small pan with the water and cook
over a low heat, stirring with a wooden
spoon until the jelly has dissolved.
Brush this over the strawberries.

Tip

Placing scrunched up foil in
each pastry case prevents
them from shrinking.

Chocolate tart

This is perfect for chocoholics! This chocolate tart has a tangy orange pastry base. It can be served warm or cold with a dollop of ice cream or cream.

20 mins   45 mins   Serves 8

Ingredients

- 350g (12oz) ready-prepared shortcrust pastry
- 4tbsp orange marmalade
- 200g (7oz) milk chocolate (broken into pieces)
- 2 large eggs (beaten)
- 50g (2oz) caster sugar
- 150ml (¼pt) double cream
- cocoa powder (for dusting)

Equipment

- rolling pin
- 23cm (9in) loose bottomed flan tin
- fork
- baking paper
- baking beans or aluminium foil
- baking tray
- metal spoon
- heatproof bowl
- small saucepan
- large mixing bowl
- electric or hand whisk
- wooden spoon
- oven gloves

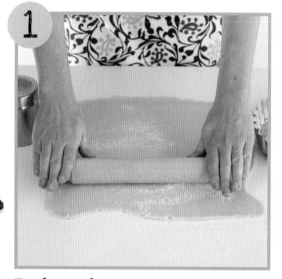

1

Preheat the oven to 190°C (375°F/ Gas 5). Using a rolling pin, roll out the pastry on a lightly floured surface and use it to line the flan tin. Chill for 15 minutes.

2

Prick the base with a fork, line with baking paper and fill with baking beans or scrunched up aluminium foil. Place on the baking tray and bake on the top shelf of the oven for 15 minutes.

3

Remove the paper and beans from the case and return it to the oven for a further 5 minutes, until golden. Whilst the pastry is still warm, spread the base with the marmalade.

4

Reduce the oven temperature to 160°C (325°F/Gas 3). Melt the chocolate in a heatproof bowl, over a saucepan of simmering water, whilst stirring. Allow to cool slightly.

5

...n a large mixing bowl, ...ace the eggs and sugar and whisk ...ith an electric or hand whisk until ...le and fluffy. Whisk in the ...ocolate until thoroughly combined.

6

Stir in the cream with a wooden spoon. Pour the mixture into the tart case. Bake for about 25–30 minutes on the top shelf of the oven until the tart has just started to set.

7

Remove the tart from the oven. It will continue to set as it cools. Dust with cocoa powder. Serve in slices with a scoop of vanilla ice cream, pouring cream or crème frâiche.

Chocolate profiterôles

You won't be able to resist these light and fluffy profiterôles. Topped with warm chocolate sauce, they're simply delicious!

Preheat the oven to 200°C (400°F/Gas 6). Grease a baking sheet and sprinkle it with a little cold water. (This will generate steam in the oven and help the choux pastry to rise.)

Place the butter and cold water in a medium saucepan and heat gently until the butter has melted. Then turn up the heat and bring them quickly to the boil.

Remove the saucepan from the heat and add all the flour at once. Then beat the melted butter and flour together with a wooden spoon until the mixture comes together.

25 mins 25 mins Serves 6

Ingredients

- 150ml (¼pt) cold water
- 50g (2oz) butter (diced)
- 75g (3oz) plain flour (sifted)
- 2 medium eggs (beaten)

For the filling

- ½tsp vanilla extract
- 300ml (½pt) double cream

For the chocolate sauce

- 125g (4oz) plain chocolate (broken into small pieces)

- 25g (1oz) butter
- 2tbsp golden syrup

Equipment

- baking sheet
- 2 medium saucepans
- wooden spoon
- dessert spoon

- oven gloves
- knife
- electric or hand whisk
- large mixing bowl
- teaspoon
- heatproof bowl

llow the mixture to cool r a couple of minutes. Then beat the eggs with an electric whisk wooden spoon, a little at a ne, until the mixture becomes ooth and shiny.

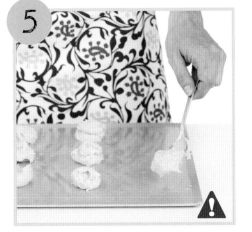

Use a dessert spoon to place 12 golf ball-sized balls of the pastry on to the baking sheet. Bake the profiterôles at the top of the oven for 20–25 minutes.

Using oven gloves, take the cooked profiterôles out of the oven. Make a slit in the side of each with a knife to let the steam out, taking care not to burn your fingers. Allow to cool.

dd the vanilla extract d the cream to a large bowl. hip them to form soft peaks using e electric or hand whisk. Then e the teaspoon to spoon the eam into the buns.

Place the chocolate, butter, and golden syrup into a heatproof bowl. Place the bowl over a saucepan of simmering water and gently melt the contents. Stir well.

Carefully spoon the chocolate sauce over the profiterôles with a dessert spoon. Then serve immediately with any remaining sauce.

Mint chocolate pots

These luxury, rather grown-up, desserts are super-chocolatey but with a minty kick. Dress them up with a stencilled shape of icing sugar or cocoa.

45 mins, plus chilling | 45-60 mins | Serves 4

Ingredients

- 300ml (10fl oz) double cream
- small bunch of mint, chopped
- 120ml (4fl oz) milk
- 175g (6oz) milk chocolate, broken into small pieces
- 3 egg yolks
- 1tbsp icing sugar, plus extra for dusting
- cocoa powder, for dusting, optional

Equipment

- chopping board
- sharp knife
- 2 saucepans
- mixing bowl
- wooden spoon
- whisk
- sieve
- roasting tin
- 4 ramekins
- card, pencil, scissors

Preheat the oven to 150°C (300°F/ Gas 2). Pour the cream into a small pan, and add the mint. Heat gently until nearly boiling, then remove from heat, cover, and leave for 30 minutes.

Meanwhile, pour the milk into another small pan and heat gently. Remove from the heat and stir in the chocolate pieces until melted and the mixture is smooth.

Whisk the egg yolks and sugar together and add the chocolatey milk and the minty cream. Mix well, then strain the mixture through a fine sieve to remove the mint.

Pour the mixture into 4 ramekins stood in a roasting tin. Add hot water until it's halfway up the outside of the cups. Bake for 45–60 minutes. Let them cool and then refrigerate for a few hour. Decorate just before serving, if you wan

Stencils

Make a stencil out of card – stars, circles, and flowers work well – and sift some icing sugar, or cocoa powder, on top for a knock-out decoration.

Meringue crowns

These beautiful desserts are impressive and the good news is they are easier to make than they look! Each crown is large, and serves 2 people, so invite your friends round to share in the sweetness.

Ingredients

- 3 eggs
- 175g (6oz) caster sugar
- a pinch of salt

For the filling

- 150ml (5fl oz) double cream, whipped (optional)
- 1 nectarine
- 1 mango
- 1 kiwi

Equipment

- baking sheet
- baking parchment
- large bowl
- electric whisk
- tablespoon
- metal mixing spoon
- piping bag
- oven gloves
- chopping board
- sharp knife
- large mixing bowl

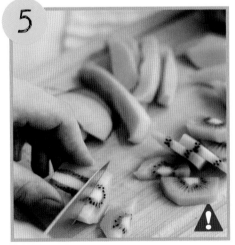

Berry-tastic

You can put any type of fruit into the meringue's centre. Try a berry medley of blueberries, raspberries, and strawberries.

1ine a baking sheet with
king parchment and ask an adult
preheat the oven to 110°C
25°F/Gas ¼). Separate the egg
hites from the yolks.

2 Whisk the egg whites
and salt in a large bowl (using
an electric whisk is easier),
until they form stiff peaks.

3 When the egg whites are
iff, whisk 5 tablespoons of the
easured sugar into the mixture,
tablespoon at a time. Then, fold
e remaining sugar into the
ixture, using a metal spoon.

4 Draw 3 circles of 10cm (4in)
diameter (a saucer works well) onto
the parchment. Using a piping bag,
squeeze out the mixture in a spiral.
Pipe small peaks to create a crown.
Three meringues fit on a sheet.

5 Towards the end of the
meringue's baking time (on the
bottom shelf for 2 hours), whip
the cream till firm (if using) and
carefully slice your fruit, and fill
the centre of each crown.

10 mins | 1 hr 30 mins | Makes 15

Ingredients

- 2 large egg whites
- 100g (3½oz) caster sugar
- 2tsp cocoa powder (plus some extra for dusting)
- 150ml (¼pt) double cream
- 1tsp peppermint extract (optional)
- 1–2 drops green food colouring (optional)
- 50g (2oz) milk or plain chocolate chips

Equipment

- 2 large baking sheets
- baking paper
- large mixing bowl
- electric or hand whisk
- metal tablespoon
- sieve
- teaspoon
- oven gloves

Preheat the oven to 140°C (275°F/Gas 1). Lightly grease 2 large baking sheets and line with baking paper. Whisk the egg whites in a bowl until they form stiff peaks.

Add the sugar to the egg whites a tablespoon at a time, whisking well with the electric or hand whisk after each spoonful. The mixture should be smooth, thick and glossy.

Sift the cocoa powder over the egg white and sugar mixture. Use a metal tablespoon to fold it over a few times until the mixture is streaky.

Using a teaspoon place heaps of the mixture onto the prepared baking sheets, spaced a little apart, until you have 30 meringues. Flatten each slightly with the back of the spoon.

Bake in the preheated oven for 1½ hours, or until the meringues peel away from the baking paper without much resistance. Leave them to cool on the baking sheets.

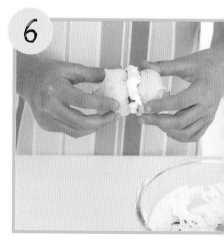

Whisk the cream, colouring and peppermint extract until thick. Stir in the chocolate chips. Spread the mixture on half of the meringues and sandwich with the other halves. Dust with cocoa.

Cocoa mint meringues

These delicious, cocoa-dusted meringues will melt in your mouth – they're crisp on the outside and soft in the middle! They are filled with lightly whipped peppermint cream and chocolate chips.

Lemon meringue

This family favourite has crunchy pastry layered with a tangy lemon filling and a soft meringue topping. It's a taste sensation!

Preheat the oven to 190°C (375°F/Gas 5). Roll out the pastry with a rolling pin on a lightly floured surface to about 25cm (10in). Line the flan tin with the pastry and chill for 15 minutes.

Prick the pastry case base with a fork, line with baking paper and fill with baking beans or scrunched aluminium foil. Place on a baking tray and bake for 15 minutes.

Remove the paper and bea from the pastry case and return to the oven for a further 5 minutes until golden. Then reduce the ove to 150°C (300°F/Gas 2).

 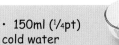 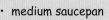

10 mins   55 mins   Serves 6

Ingredients

- 175g (6oz) ready-prepared shortcrust pastry
- 3tbsp cornflour

- 150ml (¼pt) cold water
- 2 large lemons
- 75g (3oz) caster sugar
- 25g (1oz) butter
- 2 large egg yolks

For the topping

- 2 large egg whites
- 100g (3½oz) caster sugar

Equipment

- rolling pin
- 19cm (7½in) loose-bottomed round fluted tin
- fork
- baking paper
- baking beans or aluminium foil
- baking tray
- oven gloves

- medium saucepan
- grater
- sharp knife
- chopping board
- jug
- wooden spoon
- large mixing bowl
- electric or hand whisk
- tablespoon
- heatproof bowl

4

Mix the cornflour and water together in the saucepan. Grate the zest from the lemons, then cut them in half and squeeze the juice into a jug, until you have 150ml (¼pt).

5

Add the lemon zest and juice to the saucepan, then slowly bring to the boil, stirring continuously with a wooden spoon. Simmer, still stirring, until the mixture thickens.

6

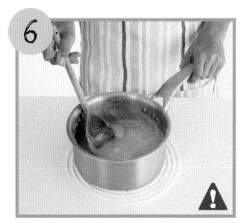

Remove the saucepan from the heat and stir in the sugar and butter. Let the mixture cool slightly, then beat in the egg yolks. Pour the mixture into the pastry case.

7

In a clean mixing bowl, whisk the egg whites with an electric or hand whisk until they form stiff peaks. Then whisk in the sugar 1tbsp at a time, until the mixture is thick and glossy.

8

Spoon the meringue mixture over the lemon mixture, leaving the rim of the pastry uncovered. Make peaks in the meringue with the back of the spoon, if you like.

9

Place the pie on the top shelf of the oven and bake for 30–35 minutes, or until the meringue is crisp and golden. Serve cold or warm with cream or ice cream.

Raspberry crème brûlée

This traditional French dessert is fun to make and eat.
Crème brûlée means "burnt cream" and it gets its name from the
burnt (caramelized) sugar on top.

10 mins, 30 mins Serves 6
plus setting time

Ingredients

- 200g (7oz) fresh raspberries
- 4 large egg yolks
- 5 tbsp golden caster sugar
- 560ml (18fl oz) double cream
- 1 tsp vanilla extract

Equipment

- 6 ramekins
- electric hand whisk
- tablespoon
- teaspoon
- small saucepan
- baking tray
- wooden spoon

1

Divide the raspberries equally among the ramekins. Whisk the egg yolks and two tablespoons of sugar in a bowl until pale and creamy.

2

Heat the cream gently (don't bo for 5 minutes. Remove from the heat, stir in the vanilla, and allow to cool for 5 minutes. Slowly add the warm cream to the egg mixture, whisking constantly.

3

Pour the mixture back into the pan, and cook over a low heat (do not boil) for a few minutes, stirring constantly. If overheated, the custard will curdle. Pour the custard into the ramekins and allow to cool.

4

Transfer to the refrigerator t set for 2 hours. Sprinkle the custards evenly with the remaining sugar. Place under a hot grill until the sugar bubbles and browns. Allow the topping to harde for 20 minutes before serving.

Variation

Use ripe peaches or sweet cherries instead of the raspberries for an alternative flavour.

Rhubarb cobblers

A cobbler is a cooked fruit pudding

with a topping that resembles a scone, or a dumpling. Often, it's made in one large dish, but this recipe is for four individual cobblers.

1 hour, plus sitting time | 25-30 mins | Serves 4

Ingredients

- 350g (12oz) rhubarb, cut into 2cm (³/₄in) pieces
- grated rind of 1 orange
- 50g (1³/₄oz) soft brown sugar
- 1tbsp cornflour
- 175g (6oz) self-raising flour
- 50g (1³/₄oz) butter, cut into cubes
- 50g (1³/₄oz) caster sugar, plus a little for sprinkling
- 120ml (4fl oz) milk, plus extra for brushing

Equipment

- sharp knife
- mixing bowls
- wooden spoon
- round biscuit cutter
- 4 ramekins
- pastry brush

Preheat the oven to 180°C (350°F/ gas 4). Put the rhubarb, orange rind, sugar, and cornflour in a bowl and stir together. Let the fruit sit for 10–15 minutes.

Meanwhile make the topping: put the flour in a large bowl, then add the butter. Use your fingertips to rub the butter into the flour until the mixture looks like fine breadcrumbs.

Stir in the sugar, then add the milk, a little at a time, until you have a slightly sticky, soft dough.

Transfer the dough to a lightly floured surface and pat it out until it's 1cm (½in) thick. Cut the dough into 8 rounds.

Divide the rhubarb between 4 oven-proof dishes. Put 2 scones on top of each. Brush with milk and sprinkle with sugar. Cook on a baking tray for 25–30 minutes, until golden.

179

CAKES AND MUFFINS

Savoury muffins

Cheese and courgette give these savoury muffins a perfect for a mid-morning snack or try one as part of your packed lunch!

Tip

To make spinach and cheese muffins, replace the grated courgette with 180g (6oz) chopped baby spinach leaves in step 3.

10 mins | 25 mins | Makes 12

Ingredients

- 2 medium-sized courgettes
- 125g (4oz) mature hard cheese (such as Cheddar)
- 275g (10oz) plain flour
- 1tbsp baking powder
- 1tbsp caster sugar
- 1tsp salt
- ½tsp ground black pepper
- 2 medium eggs (beaten)
- 175ml (6floz) milk
- 85g (3oz) lightly salted butter (melted)

Equipment

- 2 x 6-hole or 12-hole muffin tin
- 12 muffin cases
- grater
- large mixing bowl
- sieve
- metal spoon
- jug
- fork or whisk
- oven gloves
- cooling rack

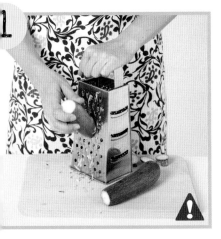

1 Preheat the oven to 375°F (190°C/Gas 5). Line a muffin tin with 12 paper muffin cases. Trim the ends off the courgettes and grate them coarsely. Then grate the cheese.

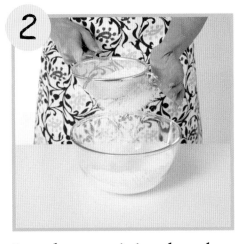

2 In a large mixing bowl, sift together the flour and the baking powder. Stir in the sugar, salt, and pepper with a metal spoon until they are thoroughly mixed together.

3 Add most of the grated cheese (but save a little to sprinkle over the top) and grated courgette. Using the metal spoon, mix well to combine all the ingredients.

4 In a jug, beat together the eggs, milk and butter with a fork or whisk. Pour them into the large mixing bowl and stir until just combined. The batter should be lumpy.

5 Using the metal spoon, divide the mixture equally between the 12 muffin cases and sprinkle each one with the remaining grated cheese.

6 Place the muffins in the centre of the oven and bake for 20–25 minutes until risen, golden and firm. Leave to cool on a cooling rack before serving them warm or cold.

Ingredients

- 280g (10oz) plain flour
- 1tbsp baking powder
- 1tsp salt
- 1tsp mustard powder
- 125g (4½oz) mature Cheddar cheese, grated
- 2tbsp chopped fresh parsley
- 1tbsp chopped fresh oregano
- 2tsp chopped fresh thyme
- freshly ground black pepper
- 2 eggs
- 200ml (7fl oz) semi-skimmed milk
- 75g (2½oz) butter, melted

Equipment

- muffin tin
- paper muffin cases
- sieve
- mixing bowls
- sharp knife
- chopping board
- cheese grater
- fork
- wooden spoon

Herby cheese muffins

Here is a herby muffin recipe that uses parsley, oregano, and thyme. The muffins are irresistible and best eaten the day they're made, although they will last for a couple of days if you keep them in a tin.

Preheat the oven to 190°C (375°F/ Gas 5). Line a muffin tin with 10 paper muffin cases. Then sieve the flour, baking powder, and salt into a bowl.

Add the mustard, three quarters of the cheese, and the parsley, oregano, and thyme. Season with black pepper and mix everything together.

In another bowl, beat together the eggs, milk, and melted butter, and pour over the dry ingredients.

Stir the mixture until everything is just combined. Your batter should be quite lumpy.

5

Spoon the batter into the muffin cases, then sprinkle the rest of the cheese on top. Bake for 20–25 minutes until risen and firm.

Variation

Basil and tomato muffins
To make these, simply follow the main recipe, but swap the herbs for 2tbsp chopped fresh basil, and stir in 75g (2½oz) chopped sun-dried tomatoes.

Ingredients

- 140g (5oz) plain flour
- 2tsp baking powder
- ½tsp bicarbonate of soda
- 85g (3oz) light brown sugar
- 50g (1³/₄oz) roasted hazelnuts, chopped
- 100g (3½oz) carrot, grated
- 100g (3½oz) unsulphured apricots, chopped finely
- 1tbsp poppy seeds
- ½tsp ground cinnamon
- 100g (3½oz) porridge oats
- zest of 2 oranges
- 200ml (7fl oz) buttermilk or milk and 1 tbsp lemon juice
- 1 egg, beaten
- 3tbsp melted butter
- a pinch of salt
- juice of 1 large orange

For the topping

- 2tbsp soft brown sugar
- 50g (1½oz) porridge oats
- 1 tbsp melted butter

Equipment

- small glass bowl
- baking sheet
- chopping board
- sharp knife
- large glass bowl
- spoon
- muffin cases
- muffin tray

Carrot and orange muffins

The versatile carrot can be savoury or sweet, as in these delicious muffins – a perfect snack or lunchbox treat.

Preheat the oven to 200°C (400°F/ Gas 6). To make the topping, mix together the ingredients in a bowl. Sprinkle the mixture onto a baking sheet. Bake for 5 minutes, then leave to cool.

In a large bowl, mix the flour, baking powder, bicarbonate of soda, and sugar. Then, add the nuts, carrot, apricot, poppy seeds, cinnamon, oats, and orange zest. Mix together well.

In another bowl, use a spoon to mix the buttermilk, egg, butter, salt, and orange juice. Pour this liquid mixture onto the bowl of dry ingredients.

Stir the two mixtures together using a spoon. Be careful not to over mix as this will "knock out" all the air. In fact, the lumpier the mixture, the better the muffins will be!

5

lace 8 paper cases into a muffin
ay. Spoon the mixture into the cases,
ling them two-thirds full.

6

prinkle the crumbly
pping over the muffins. Bake in
e preheated oven for about
–30 minutes until well risen
d golden. Leave to cool.

Mini muffins

These bite-sized treats have the delicious combination of tasty banana and melt-in-your-mouth chocolate chips. They are perfect for lunch boxes or for a light snack.

10 mins 12 mins Makes 48

Ingredients

- 280g (10oz) plain flour
- 1tbsp baking powder
- ½tsp salt
- 125g (4oz) caster sugar
- 2 large ripe bananas (peeled and roughly chopped)
- 1 large egg
- 240ml (8floz) milk
- 85g (3oz) butter (melted)
- 175g (6oz) milk chocolate chips or chunks

Equipment

- 24-hole mini-muffin tin
- mini-muffin paper cases (optional)
- large mixing bowl
- sieve
- wooden spoon
- small mixing bowl
- fork
- small hand whisk
- jug
- teaspoon
- oven gloves

1

Preheat the oven to 200°C (400°F/Gas 6). Grease a 24-hole mini-muffin tin with butter (or line it with mini-muffin paper cases) to stop the muffins from sticking.

2

In a large mixing bowl, sift together the flour, baking powder, and salt. Stir in the sugar with a wooden spoon until all the ingredients are thoroughly mixed.

3

In a small mixing bowl, mash the 2 bananas with a fork until nearly smooth but with a few lumps remaining – this will give a nice texture to the muffins.

4

In a jug, whisk together the egg, milk and butter, then pour onto the mashed banana in the bowl. Stir the ingredients together until they are combined thoroug

5

dd the egg and banana
ixture to the flour mixture. Stir the
gredients together with a wooden
oon to just combine, then fold in
e chocolate chips or chunks.

6

Spoon the mixture into the tin
and bake for 10–12 minutes. Leave the
cakes to cool in the tin then remove
them and repeat with the remaining
ingredients to make a second batch.

Variation

Try using white chocolate
chips or chunks in step 5
instead of milk chocolate
chips. You could also
experiment with other
flavours of chocolate.

Cupcakes

Cook these pretty cakes and decorate with pastel colour icings, sweets or crystallised flowers. Stack in a tower as an alternative way to celebrate a birthday party or naming day.

Tip

These cakes can be made the day before and stored in an airtight container.

Ingredients

- 150g (5½oz) unsalted butter, softened
- 150g (5½oz) caster sugar
- 150g (5½oz) self-raising flour
- 3 medium eggs, whisked
- ½tsp vanilla extract

30 mins | 15 mins | Makes 20

For the icing and decoration

- 225g (8oz) icing sugar, sifted
- 2-3tbsp hot water
- 3 different food colourings
- edible crystallised flowers, sugar strands, hundreds and thousands or sweets

Equipment

- 2 x12 bun tins
- 20 paper cases
- 2 mixing bowls
- wooden spoon
- 2 metal spoons
- cooling rack
- knife
- 3 small mixing bowls

1 Preheat the oven to 180°C, (350°F/Gas 4). Line 2 x 12 bun tins with 20 paper cases.

2 Place the butter, sugar, self-raising flour, eggs, and vanilla extract in a bowl and beat with a wooden spoon until pale and creamy.

3 Divide between the paper cases. Bake for 15 minutes until golden and just firm. Cool in the tin for 5 minutes, then transfer to a cooling rack to cool.

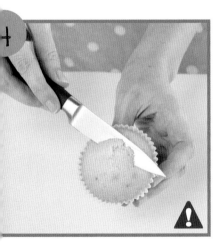

4 Carefully trim any pointed tops to make a flat surface. Put the cupcakes to one side.

5 Place the icing in a large bowl, gradually beat in sufficient water to give a smooth thick icing, which coats the back of a spoon.

6 Transfer the icing mixture to 3 individual bowls and add a few drops of food colouring to each. Spoon onto the cakes and top with decorations. Allow to set.

Lime and coconut cupcakes

Give classic cupcakes a makeover with mouthwatering coconut and refreshing lime.

 10 mins   20 mins   Makes 18

Ingredients

- 125g (4oz) butter (softened)
- 125g (4oz) caster sugar
- finely grated zest and juice of 2 limes
- 2 medium eggs
- 150g (5oz) self-raising flour
- 1tsp baking powder
- 50g (2oz) sweetened and tenderised or desiccated coconut
- finely grated zest and juice of 1 lime
- 175g (6oz) icing sugar
- few drops green colouring (optional)
- 2tbsp sweetened and tenderised or desiccated coconut

Equipment

- 12-hole bun tin
- 6-hole bun tin
- 18 paper cases
- large mixing bowl
- electric or hand whisk
- metal spoon
- oven gloves
- cooling rack
- small mixing bowl
- sieve
- teaspoon

Preheat the oven to 180°C (350°F/Gas 4). Line the bun tins with 18 paper cases. Use two 12-hole bun tins if you don't have a 6-hole tin or cook the cupcakes in batches.

In a large mixing bowl, whisk the butter, sugar, and lime zest together using an electric or hand whisk until they are light and fluffy. Whisk in the eggs and lime juice.

Using a metal spoon, fold the flour, baking powder, and coconut into the butter and sugar mixture. Divide the mixture between the paper cases. They should be about two-thirds full.

Cook the cupcakes in the oven for 15–20 minutes until well risen and golden (cook them on the top shelf if you are cooking in batches). Transfer to a cooling rack and allow to cool.

 **lace two-thirds of the me zest** (saving some for ecoration) and lime juice in a bowl d sift over the icing sugar. Stir til smooth, adding a little green blouring if you are using it.

Use a teaspoon to drizzle the icing over the tops of the cooled cupcakes and sprinkle over the coconut. Add the saved curls of lime zest to decorate.

Variation

Instead of lime zest and juice, add 2tsp vanilla extract in step 2. Stir a little vanilla extract and water in Step 5 instead of lime zest and juice.

10 mins 20 mins Makes 18

Ingredients

- 175g (6oz) butter (softened)
- 175g (6oz) caster sugar
- 175g (6oz) self-raising flour
- 2tsp mixed spice
- 2 large eggs
- grated zest of 1 orange and 1tbsp juice
- 2 medium carrots (peeled and coarsely grated)
- 50g (2oz) brazil or walnuts toasted and chopped (optional)

For the frosting

- 200g (7oz) light cream cheese
- 2tbsp icing sugar
- 1tbsp orange juice
- 2tsp grated orange zest

Equipment

- bun tin
- 18 paper cases
- large mixing bowl
- electric or hand whisk
- sieve
- dessert spoon
- oven gloves
- cooling rack
- wooden spoon
- medium bowl

Carrot cupcakes

The grated carrots make these individual cakes perfectly moist and the yummy cream cheese frosting is a deliciously tangy topping.

Preheat the oven to 180°C, (350°F/ Gas 4). Place 18 paper cases in a bun tin. Most bun tins only have 12 holes so you may have to use 2 tins or cook your cakes in batches.

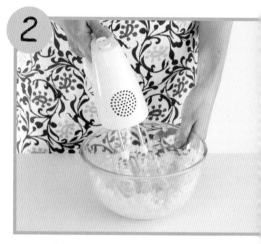

In a large mixing bowl, beat together the butter and sugar until they become pale and fluffy. Use an electric whisk if you have one. If not, then use a hand whisk.

Sift the flour and mixed spice into the bowl. Then add the eggs, orange juice, and zest. Whisk together until all the ingredients are completely combined.

Stir the grated carrots and nuts (if you are using them) into the mixing bowl. Divide the mixture equally between the 18 paper cases using a dessert spoon.

5 Bake for 18–20 minutes

n the middle of the oven until risen
nd golden brown. Remove from the
ven using the oven gloves, and place
n a cooling rack to cool completely.

6 Beat together all the frosting

ingredients with a wooden spoon.
Spread the frosting over the cooled
cakes and decorate the cupcakes
with extra orange zest.

Ingredients

- 125g (4oz) unsalted butter (softened) + extra for greasing
- 125g (4oz) soft light brown sugar
- 2 eggs (beaten)
- 200g (7oz) self-raising flour
- 1 pinch of salt
- 1tsp of baking powder
- 500g (1lb) ripe bananas (peeled and mashed)
- 2tbsp of buttermilk or natural yoghurt

For the topping

- 200g (7oz) cream cheese (room temperature)
- 60g (2oz) desiccated coconut
- 60g (2oz) icing sugar (sifted)

Equipment

- pencil
- square cake tin (20cm/8in)
- non-stick baking parchment
- scissors
- 2 large mixing bowls
- electric whisk
- sieve
- wooden spoon
- step palette knife
- oven gloves
- medium frying pan
- wooden spatula
- plate
- cooling rack

Banana Squares

The melt-in-your mouth texture of this cake is du to the creaming and folding and the use of buttermilk (or yoghurt) which make the mixture light and airy. Adding the fresh banana in step 3 also makes the cake deliciously moist.

1

Preheat the oven to 180°C (350°F/ Gas 4). With a pencil, draw round the tin onto the parchment paper. Cut out the square. Grease and line the tin.

2

Cream the butter and sugar together in a large bowl until light and fluffy. Gradually beat the eggs into the creamed butter and sugar mixture.

3

Sieve the flour, salt, and baking powder into the creamed mixture and gently fold them in. Next, stir in the banana and buttermilk.

4

Spoon the cake mixture into the prepared tin and smooth the top wit a palette knife. Bake the cake in the ove for 35 minutes, or until firm.

Meanwhile, dry fry the coconut over a low heat until golden, stirring continuously. Tip the toasted coconut onto a plate to stop it from burning.

Beat the cheese and icing sugar together with a wooden spoon until completely combined. It should become smooth, soft, and spreadable.

When the cake is completely cool, cut it into squares. Add a spoonful of the cream cheese topping and a sprinkling of toasted coconut to each square.

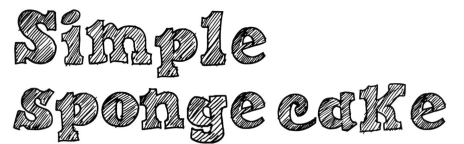

Simple Sponge cake

This cake is wonderfully light and moist.
You can also make fairy cakes with this recipe
– see the variation.

Variation

This mixture will also
make 20 fairy cakes, simply
divide the mixture between
paper cake cases and bake
for 15 minutes.

 10 mins   30 mins   Serves 6-8

Ingredients

- 175g (6oz) butter (softened)
- 175g (6oz) caster sugar
- 3 medium eggs (beaten)
- 1tsp vanilla extract

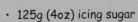

- 175g (6oz) self-raising flour
- 1tsp baking powder
- 4tbsp raspberry or strawberry jam
- icing sugar (for dusting)

For the buttercream

- 50g (2oz) butter (softened)
- 125g (4oz) icing sugar
- ½tsp vanilla extract
- 2tsp milk

Equipment

- 2 x 20cm (8in) round cake tins
- baking paper
- large mixing bowl
- sieve
- electric or hand whisk
- tablespoon
- oven gloves
- cooling rack
- mixing bowl
- wooden spoon
- spatula

1

Preheat the oven to 180°C (350°F/Gas 4). Grease two 20cm (8in) round cake tins and line each base with baking paper so that the sponge cakes don't stick.

2

Place the butter, sugar, eggs, and vanilla extract in a large bowl and sift over the flour and baking powder. Using an electric or hand whisk, beat all the ingredients together until thick.

3

Divide the mixture between the two tins, levelling the tops with the back of a tablespoon. Bake in the centre of the oven for 25–30 minutes, or until risen and firm to the touch.

4

Leave the cakes to cool in the tins for a few minutes, then turn them out onto a cooling rack. Peel off the baking paper and allow the cakes to cool completely.

5

To make the buttercream place the butter, icing sugar, vanilla extract, and milk in a mixing bowl. Beat them together with a wooden spoon until smooth and creamy.

6

Spread the flat side of one of the cakes with the jam. Spread the flat side of the other with the buttercream, then sandwich the two halves together. Dust with icing sugar.

Variation

When strawberries aren't in season (or if you fancy trying something different), try using 175g (6oz) of peaches or apricots from a can. Make sure you drain the peaches or apricots from the juices that they are preserved in.

Strawberry cake

Make this delicious cake for a family party or for a friend's birthday. You'll have lots of fun filling it with strawberries and decorating it with icing sugar.

Preheat the oven to 180°C (350°F/Gas 4). Line the tins with baking parchment. Mix the butter and sugar with an electric hand whisk until light and creamy.

Whisk in the eggs a little at a time, then sift in the flour and fold it in gently with a metal spoon.

Divide the mixture between the tins and bake for 25 minutes. Cool briefly in tins then turn out onto a wire rack to cool.

Whisk the cream in a bowl. Put the strawberries and cream on one cake. Place the other cake on top. Dust thickly with icing sugar.

20 mins   25 mins   Serves 10

Ingredients

- 225g (8oz) butter, at room temperature
- 225g (8oz) caster sugar
- 4 large eggs, lightly beaten
- 225g (8oz) self-raising flour
- icing sugar, to dust

For the filling:

- 100ml (3½oz) double cream
- 175g (6oz) strawberries, hulled and sliced

Equipment

- 2 x 20cm (8in) round sandwich tins
- electric hand whisk
- baking parchment

Lemon and lime cake

The lemon and lime juice make this cake scrumptiously moist and full of flavour. The runny glacé icing adds an extra sweetness. Share it with your family and friends.

15 mins   60 mins   Serves 12

Ingredients

- 175g (6oz) butter, at room temperature
- 175g (6oz) caster sugar
- 3 large eggs, lightly beaten
- grated zest of 1 lemon
- grated zest of 1 lime
- 2tbsp lemon juice
- 175g (6oz) self-raising flour
- 2tbsp poppy seeds (optional)
- 1 tbsp lime juice
- 100g (3½oz) icing sugar

Equipment

- electric whisk
- large mixing bowl
- loaf tin
- baking parchment
- sieve
- spatula
- cooling rack
- small mixing bowl
- spoon

1

Preheat the oven to 180ºC (350ºF/ Gas 4). Using an electric whisk, mix in the butter and caster sugar until light and fluffy. Line the loaf tin with baking parchment.

2

Beat in the eggs a little at a time, then gently fold in the lemon and lime zest, together with one tablespoon of the lemon juice. Sift in the flour, then fold in with the poppy seeds, if using.

3

Transfer to the tin and smooth the top. Bake for one hour, or until golden. Cool in the tin for 5 minutes, then move to a wire rack.

4

Mix the remaining lemon juice with the lime juice. Sift in the icing sugar and combine to make a runny icing. Spoon it over the cake.

Tip

Finish off your lemon and lime cake with a sprinkle of poppy seeds.

35 mins   30 mins   Serves 12

Ingredients

- 175g (6oz) butter (softened)
- 175g (6oz) soft brown sugar
- 150g (5oz) self-raising flour

- 25g (1oz) cocoa powder
- 1tsp baking powder
- ½tsp bicarbonate of soda
- 3 medium eggs (beaten)
- 100ml (3½fl oz) sour cream

For the icing

- 175g (6oz) white chocolate (broken into small pieces)

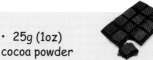

- 125g (4oz) butter
- 4tbsp milk
- 200g (7oz) icing sugar
- grated chocolate, chocolate buttons and cocoa powder for dusting (optional)

Equipment

- 2 x 20cm (8in) cake tins
- baking paper

- 2 large mixing bowls
- electric or hand whisk
- sieve
- spatula
- oven gloves
- cooling rack
- heatproof bowl
- saucepan
- wooden spoon
- palette knife

Preheat the oven to 170°C (325°F/Gas 3). Grease and line the bases of the tins with baking paper. Place the butter and sugar in a mixing bowl and whisk together until combined.

Sift over the flour, cocoa powder, baking powder, and bicarbonate of soda. Add the eggs and the sour cream and whisk with an electric or hand whisk until combined.

Divide the mixture betwee the two tins and level the tops. Ba for 25–30 minutes. Leave to cool slightly, then turn out onto a cooli rack. Remove the baking paper.

Make the icing. Place the milk, chocolate, and butter in a heatproof bowl over a saucepan of simmering water. Stir occasionally until the ingredients are melted and smooth.

Sift the icing sugar into a bowl, then pour over the melted chocolate mixture. Beat together with the whisk. Allow the icing to cool, then beat again until it forms soft peaks.

Use a little of the icing to sandwich the two cakes together. Spread the remaining icing over the top and sides of the cake. Decorate desired and dust with cocoa powde

Double chocolate fudge cake

If you are a chocolate lover, you will adore this cake! The dark chocolate sponge is filled and topped with a white chocolate icing.

Cake roll

Deliciously light sponge is combined with fruity jam in this classic cake. The technique can be tricky to master, so you might need to ask an adult to help you.

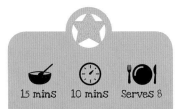
Ingredients

- 1tbsp vegetable oil
- 3 large eggs
- 125g (4oz) caster sugar, plus extra
- 125g (4oz) self-raising flour

For the filling

- 5tbsp raspberry jam

Equipment

- 33 x 23cm (13 x 9in) tin
- pastry brush
- baking paper
- large mixing bowl
- electric whisk
- sieve
- metal spoon
- oven gloves
- clean damp tea towel
- sharp knife
- palette knife

1

Preheat the oven to 200°C (400°F/ Gas 6). Brush the base and sides of a 33 x 23cm (13 x 9in) tin with a little vegetable oil, then line with baking paper. Brush with a little more oil.

2

Whisk the eggs and sugar together in a bowl, using an electric whisk. Whisk for about 10 minutes until the mixture is light and frothy and the whisk leaves a trail when lifted.

3

Sift the flour into the mixture, carefully folding at the same time with a metal spoon. Pour the mixture into the prepared tin and give it a gentle shake so that the mixture is level.

4

Place the filled tin on the top shelf of the oven. Bake for about 10 minutes or until the sponge is a golden brown and begins to shrink from the edges of the tin.

5

Lay out a damp tea tow
on the work surface. Place a piec
of baking paper a little bigger tha
the size of the tin onto the tea tov
and sprinkle it with caster sugar.

Using oven gloves, tip the warm cake out onto the sugared paper so it is upside down. Take off the gloves and gently loosen the baking paper and peel it off.

Trim the edges of the sponge with a sharp knife. Make a score mark 2.5cm (1in) from one shorter edge, being careful not to cut right through. This makes the cake easier to roll.

Leave the sponge to cool slightly, then spread the jam over it with a palette knife. Roll up the cake firmly from the cut end. Place the cake on a plate seam side down and serve in slices.

Lemon drizzle cake

It would be hard to find a more lemony cake than this one. The luscious lemon sponge has a contrasting crusty top made by pouring the lemon syrup over the cake while it is still warm.

Ingredients

- finely grated zest of 2 unwaxed lemons
- 200g (7oz) butter (softened)
- 200g (7oz) caster sugar
- 3 medium eggs (beaten)
- 200g (7oz) self-raising flour (sifted)
- syrup
- juice 4 lemons (about 100ml (3½fl oz)
- 75g (3oz) granulated sugar

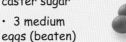

Equipment

- 20cm (8in) round springform cake tin
- baking paper
- large mixing bowl

- electric or hand whisk
- metal spoon
- oven gloves
- small mixing bowl
- cocktail stick
- cooling rack

20 mins   40 mins   Serves 8

1

reheat the oven to 180°C (350°F/Gas 4). Butter a 20cm (8in) round, springform cake tin and line the base with baking paper to prevent the cake from sticking to the tin.

2

Place the lemon zest, butter, and caster sugar in a large mixing bowl and beat until the mixture is light and fluffy. You can use an electric or hand whisk.

3

Whisk in the eggs a little at a time. If the mixture starts to curdle, add 1tbsp of the flour. Use a metal spoon to fold in the flour then spoon the mixture into the prepared tin.

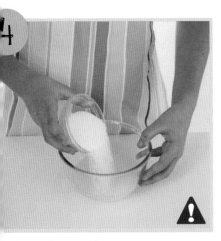

4

Bake the cake in the centre of the oven for 35–40 minutes. Put the lemon juice and granulated sugar in a small bowl. Leave in a warm place stirring occasionally.

5

When the cake has risen, and is golden and shrinking from the tin, remove it from the oven and prick all over with a cocktail stick about 20 times.

6

Drizzle the juice over the cake slowly. It will leave a crust as it sinks in. Allow the cake to cool in the tin for 10 minutes, then carefully transfer it to a cooling rack.

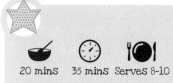

20 mins   35 mins   Serves 8-10

- 125ml (4floz) milk
- ½tsp bicarbonate of soda
- 175g (6oz) self-raising flour

For the topping

- 2 eating apples
- 50g (2oz) butter (diced)
- 50g (2oz) light muscovado sugar

- 1tsp ground cinnamon (optional)

Equipment

- 20cm (8in) round cake tin with sides 7.5cm (3in) deep
- peeler
- corer
- sharp knife
- chopping board

- small mixing bowl
- spoon
- large mixing bowl
- electric or hand whisk
- sieve
- spatula
- oven gloves

Ingredients

- 125g (4oz) butter (softened)
- 125g (4oz) caster sugar
- 2 large eggs

1

Preheat the oven to 180°C (350°F/Gas 4). Grease the base and sides of a 20cm (8in) round cake tin, 7.5cm (3in) deep. The cake tin should not be a springform or loose-bottomed one.

2

Peel the apples with a peeler, then using a corer remove the cores from the centres. Cut each apple into 5 rings and place in the bottom of the tin, overlapping if necessary.

3

In a small mixing bowl m together the diced butter, sugar (a cinnamon if you are using it) and sprinkle the mixture over the appl rings in the bottom of the cake tin

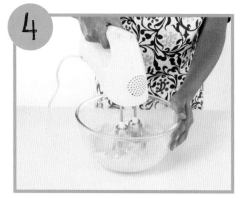

4

Place the butter and sugar in a large bowl. Using an electric or hand whisk beat them together until pale and fluffy. Whisk in the eggs, adding a little flour if the mixture starts to curdle.

5

Whisk in the milk and bicarbonate of soda a little at a time, with some of the flour. Sift over the remaining flour and stir the mixture together until they are just combined.

6

Pour the cake mixture over the apple rings and spread evenly, using a spatula. Bake the cake in the centre of the oven for 30–35 minutes, until golden and firm to the touch.

Upside-down apple cake

This fruity cake is fun to make and impressive to look at!
Rings look prettier, but slices of apple or pineapple also work.

7

⚠️

Cool the cake in the tin for 5 minutes, then turn it out. Serve the apple upside-down cake in slices. It can be eaten cold or warm with custard, cream, or ice cream.

Banana and buttermilk cake

This cake has a lovely crumbly texture combined with crunchy nuts and soft gooey banana. It is a great way to use up any ripe bananas.

15 mins | 1 hr | Serves 10

Ingredients

- 3 ripe bananas (broken into pieces)
- 1tsp lemon juice
- 100g (3½oz) pecan nut halves (optional)
- 100g (3½oz) butter (softened)
- 175g (6oz) soft brown sugar
- 2 medium eggs (beaten)
- 1tsp vanilla extract
- 250g (9oz) plain flour
- 1tsp salt
- 1tsp bicarbonate of soda
- 1tsp ground mixed spice
- 100ml (3½floz) buttermilk
- 1 small banana (sliced)

Equipment

- 900g (2lb) loaf tin
- baking paper
- 2 small bowls
- fork
- large mixing bowl
- electric or hand whisk
- sieve
- metal spoon
- aluminium foil
- cooling rack

Preheat the oven to 180°C (350°F/ Gas 4). Grease and line the base of a 900g (2lb) loaf tin with baking paper. Mash the banana pieces with the lemon juice, using a fork.

Use your hands to break the pecan halves into small pieces into a bowl if you are adding nuts. If you don't like nuts, just leave this step out.

Place the butter and sugar in a large mixing bowl. Using an electric or hand whisk, beat them together until they are combined and become light and fluffy.

Beat in the eggs and vanilla extrac a little at a time. Stir in the banana mixtu Sift in the flour, salt, bicarbonate of soda and mixed spice and stir into the mixtur with a metal spoon.

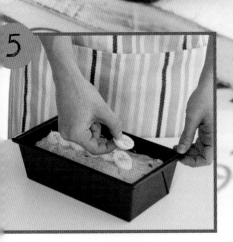

5

tir in the buttermilk. Stir in
e nuts if you are using them, saving
few. Pour the mixture into the tin
d place the sliced banana on the
p. Sprinkle over the saved nuts.

6

Bake in the oven for 50–60
minutes. If the cake becomes too
brown, cover it with foil. Allow the
cake to cool in the tin, then tip it
out onto a cooling rack and remove
the baking paper.

Variation

Replace the pecan nuts
with chopped walnuts or
brazil nuts or just leave
them out.

Marble cake

Chocolate and orange cake mixtures are swirled together to make this spectacular marble-effect cake. This cake is lots of fun to make and you can change your swirling patterns every time you make it! Serve it cold or hot with custard or cream. Delicious!

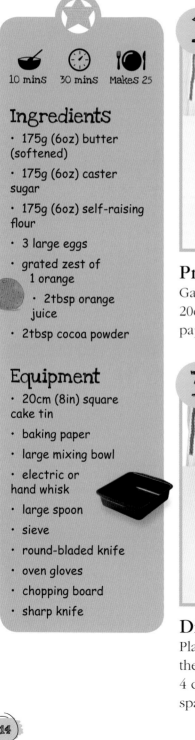

10 mins   30 mins   Makes 25

Ingredients

- 175g (6oz) butter (softened)
- 175g (6oz) caster sugar
- 175g (6oz) self-raising flour
- 3 large eggs
- grated zest of 1 orange
- 2tbsp orange juice
- 2tbsp cocoa powder

Equipment

- 20cm (8in) square cake tin
- baking paper
- large mixing bowl
- electric or hand whisk
- large spoon
- sieve
- round-bladed knife
- oven gloves
- chopping board
- sharp knife

1

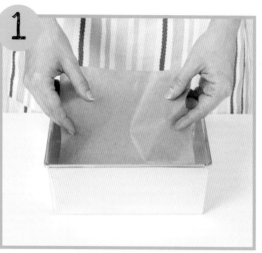

Preheat the oven to 180°C (350°F/ Gas 4). Grease and line the base of a 20cm (8in) square cake tin with baking paper to prevent the cake from sticking.

2

Place all the ingredients except the cocoa powder in a large mixing bowl. Using an electric or hand whisk, beat them all together until mixed and smooth.

3

Divide the mixture in half. Place large spoonfuls of one half of the mixture into the tin in each of the 4 corners and in the middle. Leave space between each spoonful.

4

Sift the cocoa powder over the remaining mixture in the bowl and whisk together until combined. Spoon the chocolate mixture into the spaces in the cake tin.

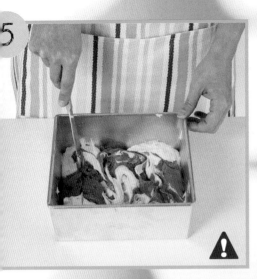

Gently drag a round-bladed knife through the mixtures to create a swirl effect with the brown and white mixtures. Don't overdo it, or you will mix the 2 colours together completely.

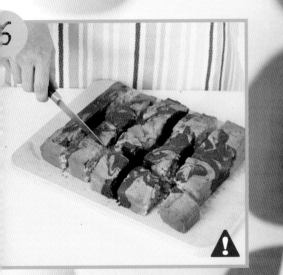

Bake the cake for 30 minutes, until well risen and springy. Allow it to cool in the tin, then remove it and peel off the baking paper. Cut it into 25 squares with a sharp knife.

Blueberry and sour cream cake

Adding sour cream makes this pretty cake wonderfully moist and creamy. It can be decorated with fresh blueberries for an extra burst of fruity flavour!

25 mins   50 mins   Serves 10

Ingredients
- 75g (3oz) butter (softened)
- 250g (9oz) caster sugar
- 284ml pot sour cream
- 2 medium eggs

- 2tsp vanilla extract
- 300g (11oz) self-raising flour
- 1tsp baking powder
- 225g (8oz) blueberries

For the frosting
- 200g (7oz) cream cheese
- finely grated zest of
  1 lemon

- 1tsp vanilla extract
- 1tbsp lemon juice
- 100g (3½oz) icing sugar
- 125g (4oz) blueberries

Equipment
- 23cm (9in) springform
  round cake tin
- baking paper

- 2 large mixing bowls
- electric or hand whisk
- sieve
- metal spoon
- cooling rack
- small bowl
- wooden spoon
- oven gloves
- palette knife

1

Preheat the oven to 180°C
(350°F/Gas 4). Grease a 23cm (9in)
round springform cake tin and line
the base with baking paper to
prevent the cake from sticking.

2

Place the butter and caster
sugar in a large mixing bowl. Using
an electric or hand whisk, cream the
butter and sugar together until they
are light and fluffy.

3

Whisk in a little of the sour
cream until the mixture is smooth.
Then whisk in the remaining sour
cream, eggs, and vanilla extract until
thoroughly combined and smooth.

4

Sift the flour and baking
powder over the mixture and
gently fold together using a metal
spoon. Gently fold in the
blueberries, then spoon the
mixture into the tin. Level the top.

5

Bake for 45–50 minutes
or until the cake feels firm. Leave
the cake to cool in the tin for 10
minutes, then tip out onto a cooling
rack and peel off the paper. Leave
to cool completely.

6

Beat the cream cheese,
lemon zest and juice with a
wooden spoon in a bowl. Sift over
the icing sugar and beat in. Spread
the frosting on the cake and
decorate with blueberries.

Tropical fruit cake

This cake is really simple to make. It uses pineapple and mango to add a tropical flavour, but you can use any of your favourite dried fruit. make it! Serve it cold or hot with custard or cream. Delicious!

15 mins   1 hr   Serves 12

Ingredients

- 250g (9oz) soft mixed dried tropical fruit e.g. pineapple, mango, papaya, apricots
- 100g (3½oz) raisins
- 1tsp mixed spice
- 125g (4oz) butter (diced)
- 125g (4oz) soft brown sugar
- 150ml (¼pt) cold water
- 225g (8oz) self-raising flour
- 1 egg (beaten)

Equipment

- 900g (2lb) loaf tin
- baking paper or loaf tin liner
- chopping board
- sharp knife
- medium saucepan
- wooden spoon
- skewer
- oven gloves

Grease and line the base of a 900g (2lb) loaf tin (or use a loaf tin liner). On a chopping board, carefully cut the tropical fruit into small pieces with a sharp knife.

Place the raisins, dried tropical fruit, mixed spice, butter, sugar, and water in a medium saucepan. Warm over a low heat until the butter has melted, stirring with a wooden spoon.

Bring the butter and fruit mixture to the boil and allow it to simmer for 5 minutes. Then remove the saucepan from the heat and leave the mixture to cool completely.

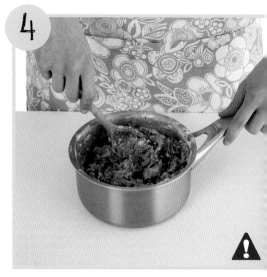

Preheat the oven to 150°C (300°F/ Gas 2). When the mixture is cool, stir in the flour and the egg with the wooden spoon until combined. Then spoon it into the prepared tin.

5

Bake in the centre of the oven for 50–60 minutes, or until a skewer inserted into the middle comes out clean. Leave the cake to cool in the tin. When cool, serve in slices.

Variation

This recipe can be made into a traditional fruit cake by replacing the tropical fruit with currants, sultanas, more raisins and glacé cherries.

15 mins, plus chilling   40 mins   Serves 8

Ingredients

- 200g (7oz) digestive biscuits
- 50g (2oz) butter
- 600g (1lb 4oz) cream cheese
- 142ml pot sour cream
- 25g (1oz) cornflour
- 75g (3oz) icing sugar (sifted)
- 3 medium eggs
- 1tsp vanilla extract
- 225g (8oz) fresh raspberries

To Serve

- fresh raspberries
- icing sugar (for dusting)

Equipment

- food bag
- rolling pin or food processor
- chopping board
- wooden spoon
- saucepan
- 20cm (8in) springform round cake tin
- large mixing bowl
- electric or hand whisk
- metal spoon
- baking tray
- oven gloves

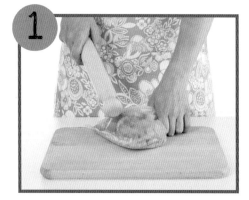

Preheat oven to 170°C (325°F/ Gas 3). Place the biscuits in a food bag and crush them with a rolling pin. (You could also do this with a food processor.).

Melt the butter in a saucepan and stir in the crushed biscuits. Press the biscuit mixture into the base of the tin with the back of a spoon. Chill in the fridge for 15 minutes.

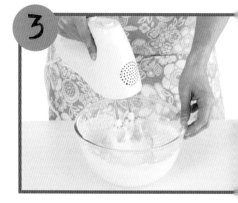

Place the cream cheese and sour cream in a large mixing bowl. Using an electric or hand whisk, beat the mixture until smooth. Then beat in the cornflour and icing sugar.

Add the eggs and vanilla extract to the bowl and whisk until smooth. Using a metal spoon, carefully stir in the raspberries. Pour this mixture over the biscuit base.

Place the cake on a baking tray and bake for 35–40 minutes in the middle of the oven until just set. Leave it to cool, then chill the cake in the fridge for 2–3 hours or overnight.

Carefully remove the cake from the springform tin and decorate with the fresh raspberries Dust the cheesecake with icing sugar, and serve it in slices.

Baked raspberry cheesecake

This baked cheesecake is so simple to make.
You could replace the raspberries with blueberries if you prefer.
Serve at a party for your friends or family.

BISCUITS, COOKIES, AND TRAYBAKES

Star biscuits

These biscuits make great gifts for your friends and family. You can use different shaped cutters for different themes, such as Christmas, Halloween, or Valentine's Day.

25 mins　50 mins　Serves 10

Ingredients

- 200g (7oz) plain flour
- 125g (4oz) butter (diced)
- 100g (3½oz) caster sugar
- 1tsp ground cinnamon
- finely grated zest of 1 orange
- 1 medium egg, lightly beaten
- 2tbsp golden syrup

To decorate

- ribbon, writing icing, edible silver balls or hundreds and thousands

Equipment

- 2 large baking sheets
- baking paper
- food processor
- small bowl
- fork
- rolling pin

- star shape cutter
- bamboo skewer
- oven gloves
- cooling rack

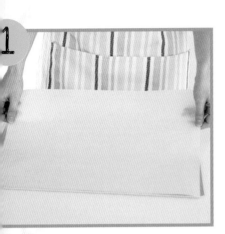

1 reheat the oven to 180°C (350°F/Gas 4). Line 2 large baking sheets with baking paper. Pulse the flour and butter in a food processor, until the mixture resembles fine breadcrumbs.

2 Add the sugar, cinnamon, and orange zest and pulse again. In a small bowl, beat together the egg and golden syrup with a fork then add this to the breadcrumb mixture.

3 Process the mixture in the food processor until it comes together in a ball. Lift the ball of dough out, wrap it in cling film and chill for 10 minutes in the fridge.

4 Roll out the chilled dough on a lightly floured surface, to 5mm (¼in) thickness. Cut into stars using a shaped cutter. Re-roll and cut out more stars until you use up all the dough.

5 Place the stars slightly apart on the baking sheets and cook for 10–12 minutes. Allow to cool for 2 minutes and if they are decorations, poke a hole in the top of each using the skewer.

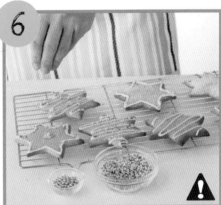

6 Transfer the stars to a cooling rack. When they are cool, decorate them as desired. Thread the holes with ribbon and tie the ends together if you are making them as decorations.

Raisin biscuits

These simply scrumptious biscuits are sure to become a favourite. They are perfect for an afternoon snack or a light dessert.

20 mins   14 mins   Makes 20

Ingredients

- 125g (4oz) butter (softened)
- 75g (3oz) caster sugar
- finely grated zest of 1 lemon
- 1 egg (separated)
- 200g (7oz) plain flour (sifted)
- 75g (3oz) raisins
- 2tbsp milk
- 1-2tbsp caster sugar (for sprinkling)

Equipment

- 2 large baking sheets
- large mixing bowl
- electric or hand whisk
- round-bladed knife
- rolling pin
- 6cm (2.5in) round fluted cutter
- oven gloves
- fork
- pastry brush
- palette knife
- cooling rack

1

Preheat the oven to 180°C (350°F/ Gas 4). Grease 2 baking sheets. In a bowl, beat the butter, sugar, and lemon zest together using an electric or hand whisk, until they are pale and fluffy.

2

Beat in the egg yolk but keep the egg white to one side. Using a round bladed knife, gently stir in the sifted flou and raisins. Gradually stir in the milk until the dough comes together.

3

Tip the dough onto a lightly floured surface and knead it gently until it is smooth and supple. Shape the dough into a ball with your hands.

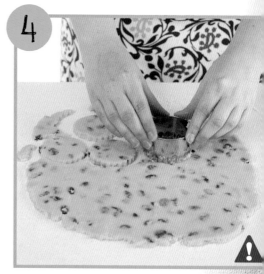

4

Roll the dough out to about 5mm (¼in) thick then cut out the biscuits usin a 6cm (2.5in) round fluted cutter. Place the biscuits on the baking sheets and bake for 8–10 minutes.

5

6

Using oven gloves, remove the baking sheets from the oven. Lightly whisk the egg white with a fork, then brush it over the biscuits with a pastry brush and sprinkle them with caster sugar.

Wearing the oven gloves, return the biscuits to the oven for 3–4 minutes until they turn golden. Once cooked, remove the biscuits from the oven and transfer them to a cooling rack.

Variation

Replace the raisins with currants if you prefer them or spice things up by adding a little cinnamon or mixed spice.

Tip

A good way to measure out golden syrup is to lightly grease the tablespoon with a little oil. You'll find the golden syrup will run off the spoon into the pan.

Coconut biscuits

Give oat biscuits a tasty tropical twist with creamy coconut. The bicarbonate of soda gives the biscuits a great crunchy texture.

10 mins | 10 mins | Makes 20

Ingredients

- 75g (3oz) desiccated coconut
- 100g (3½oz) plain flour
- 100g (3½oz) caster sugar
- 100g (3½oz) porridge oats
- 100g (3½oz) butter (diced)
- 1tbsp golden syrup
- 1tsp bicarbonate of soda
- 2tbsp hot water

Equipment

- 2 baking trays
- baking paper
- large mixing bowl
- wooden spoon
- medium saucepan
- dessert spoon
- oven gloves
- palette knife
- cooling rack

1

Preheat the oven to 180°C (350°F/Gas 4). Line 2 baking trays with baking paper. Place the coconut, flour, sugar, and oats in a mixing bowl and mix together with a wooden spoon.

2

Place the butter and golden syrup in a medium saucepan and heat over a low heat until melted. Stir the mixture with a wooden spoon to mix thoroughly.

3

Mix the bicarbonate of soda with the hot water. Add to the butter mixture in the saucepan. The bicarbonate will make the butter and golden syrup mixture fizz. Stir well.

4

Pour the butter mixture into the large mixing bowl and mix well. Spoon the mixture onto the baking trays with a dessert spoon, leaving room between each one for the biscuits to spread.

5

Bake the biscuits for 8–10 minutes on the top shelf of the oven until golden. Allow the biscuits to cool on the tray for five minutes, then transfer to a cooling rack to cool completely.

Jam shapes

These pretty jam-filled biscuits take time to make, but they are definitely worth the effort! The combination of gooey jam and crunchy biscuit is heavenly.

Ingredients

- 175g (6oz) butter (softened)
- 175g (6oz) caster sugar
- 1tsp vanilla extract
- 1tsp finely grated lemon zest
- 1 medium egg (beaten)
- 1 egg yolk
- 275g (10oz) plain flour, plus a little extra for rolling out
- 6tbsp raspberry or strawberry jam
- 2tbsp icing sugar (for dusting)

Equipment

- 2 large baking sheets
- baking paper
- food processor
- cling film
- rolling pin
- 6cm (2½in) cookie cutter
- 2–3cm (1–1½in) cookie cutter
- oven gloves
- cooling rack
- palette knife

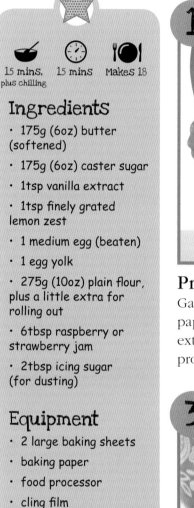

Preheat the oven to 170°C (325°F/Gas 3). Line 2 baking sheets with baking paper. Process the butter, sugar, vanilla extract, and lemon zest in a food processor until smooth.

Add the egg, egg yolk, and flour to the food processor and process again until the mixture resembles breadcrumbs and is starting to come together in a dough.

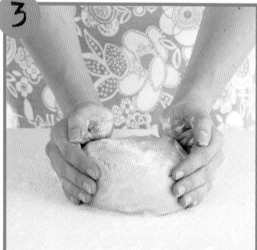

Transfer the dough to a lightly floured surface and lightly knead until it is smooth. Flatten into a circle, wrap it in cling film and chill for 30 minutes.

On a lightly floured surface, roll the dough out to 3mm (¼in) thick. Using a 6cm (2½in) cookie cutter, cut out as many biscuits as you can. You should get about 36 in total.

5 Use a **2–3cm** (1–1½in) cookie cutter to cut out the middle from 8 of the biscuits (you can bake these too if you like). Arrange on the baking sheets and chill for 15 minutes.

6 **Bake on the middle shelf** of the oven (in batches, if necessary) for about 10–12 minutes or until golden. Cool on the baking sheets for 1 minute, then transfer them to a cooling rack.

7 **When completely cool,** spread the whole biscuits with jam. Then dust icing sugar on the biscuits with holes in. Press one sugar-dusted biscuit onto each jam-covered one and serve.

Ingredients

- 350g (12oz) plain flour
- 2tsp ground ginger
- 1tsp bicarbonate of soda
- 125g (4oz) butter (diced)
- 150g (5oz) soft dark brown sugar
- 4tbsp golden syrup
- 1 medium egg (beaten)
- Sweets, currants, and icing for decoration

Equipment

- 2 large baking trays
- baking paper
- large mixing bowl
- wooden spoon
- rolling pin
- cutters of your choice
- oven gloves

1

Preheat the oven to 180°C (350°F/Gas 4). Line 2 large baking trays with baking paper. If you only have 1 tray, you will need to cook the biscuits in 2 batches.

2

Place the flour, ginger, and bicarbonate of soda in a large bowl. Stir the ingredients together with a wooden spoon until they are thoroughly mixed.

3

Rub the butter into the mixture using your fingertips. Continue rubbing in the butter until the mixture resembles fine breadcrumbs. Stir in the sugar.

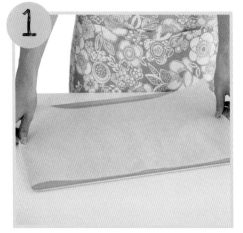

4

Stir in the golden syrup and egg, until the mixture starts to come together in a dough. Tip the dough mixture onto a lightly floured surface and knead it until smooth.

5

Roll out the dough on a lightly floured surface to a thickness of 5mm (¼in), then using your cutters, cut out the shapes. Re-roll the leftover dough and cut out more biscuits.

6

Place the biscuits on the baking trays and cook for 9–10 minutes. Allow the biscuits to cool on the trays. Decorate with sweets, currants and icing.

Gingerbread

Gingerbread tastes great and smells wonderful as it bakes. This recipe can be used for regular shaped biscuits, pretty tree decorations or gingerbread people

Melting moments

These melt-in-the-mouth biscuits are a chocolate-lover's dream! The creamy filling and crunchy biscuit is a tasty combination.

20 mins　15 mins　Makes 15

Ingredients

- 175g (6oz) butter (softened)
- 50g (2oz) caster sugar
- 1tsp vanilla extract

- 125g (4oz) plain flour
- 25g (1oz) cornflour
- 25g (1oz) cocoa powder (sifted)

For the filling

- 100g (3½oz) good quality chocolate (broken into pieces)
- 2tbsp double cream

Equipment

- 2 large baking sheets
- baking paper
- large mixing bowl
- electric whisk or wooden spoon
- sieve
- metal spoon

- teaspoon
- oven gloves
- cooling rack
- palette knife
- heatproof bowl
- small saucepan
- wooden spoon

Preheat the oven to 180°C (350°F/Gas 4). Line 2 baking sheets with baking paper. Place the butter, sugar and vanilla extract in a bowl and beat with a whisk or wooden spoon.

Sift the plain flour, cornflour, and cocoa powder into the mixing bowl. Using a metal spoon, fold them into the mixture until the ingredients are well combined.

Using a teaspoon, spoon 15 x 2.5cm (1in) dollops onto each baking sheet so that you have 30in total. Allow room between each one as they will spread whilst cooking.

Bake for 12–15 minutes, or until they are just starting to become dark around the edges. Remove them from the oven and leave to cool slightly before moving to a cooling rack.

Place the chocolate and cream in a heatproof bowl over a saucepan of simmering water. Stir them until they have melted. Remove from the heat and leave to cool completely.

Spread the filling on the flat side of half of the cooled biscuits with a palette knife and sandwich each one with one of the remaining biscuits.

Orange and seed cookies

These oaty cookies are flavoured with tangy orange. The sunflower seeds are a great source of vitamins and minerals, as well as adding an extra crunch!

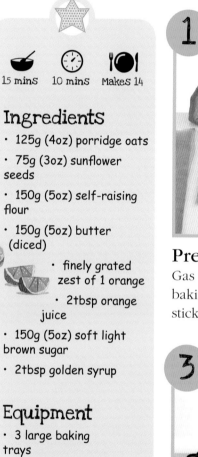

15 mins   10 mins   Makes 14

Ingredients
- 125g (4oz) porridge oats
- 75g (3oz) sunflower seeds
- 150g (5oz) self-raising flour
- 150g (5oz) butter (diced)
- finely grated zest of 1 orange
- 2tbsp orange juice
- 150g (5oz) soft light brown sugar
- 2tbsp golden syrup

Equipment
- 3 large baking trays
- baking paper
- large mixing bowl
- wooden spoon
- medium saucepan
- dessert spoon
- oven gloves
- cooling rack
- palette knife

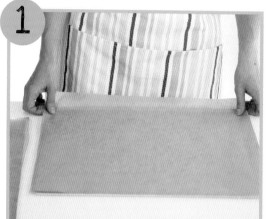

1 **Preheat the oven** to 180°C (350°F/ Gas 4). Line 3 large baking trays with baking paper to prevent the cookies from sticking to them.

2 **Place the oats,** sunflower seeds, and flour in a large mixing bowl. Stir the mixture with a wooden spoon until completely mixed together. Put the bowl to one side.

3 **Place the butter**, orange zest, juice, sugar, and golden syrup in a medium saucepan. Heat the mixture over a low heat whilst stirring, until the butter and sugar have melted.

4 **Carefully pour the butter** mixture over the ingredients in the large mixing bowl and mix them together with the wooden spoon until thoroughly combined.

lace heaped dessert
poons of the mixture onto each
ay. Leave a generous space
etween each biscuit, as they will
pread. Bake for 8–10 minutes,
ntil the cookies are golden.

Leave the cookies to cool
on the tray for a few minutes, then
transfer them to a cooling rack with
a palette knife, to become crisp.
They will keep in an airtight
container for 2–3 days.

Tip

To make smaller cookies,
place heaped teaspoons
instead of dessert spoons
of the mixture on the
trays and bake for
7–9 minutes.

Four ways with cookies

Everyone enjoys making cookies and everyone loves to eat them. Try out these tasty combinations or come up with your own.

Basic cookie dough

This recipe is for 8 people (which allows for 2 cookies each). It takes 40 mins to prepare (including chilling time) and 15 mins to cook.

- 100g (3½oz) butter, at room temperature
- 1 egg
- 125g (4½oz) caster sugar
- ½tsp vanilla extract
- 150g (5½oz) self-raising flour

Equipment

- 2 baking trays
- baking parchment
- large glass bowl
- electric whisk
- wooden spoon

① Hazelnut delights

Hazelnuts have a brilliant flavour and crunch. Alternatively, you could try the same quantity of another nut. Do you like peanuts, walnuts, pecans, or pistachios?

Ingredients

(to add to basic dough recipe above)
- 75g (2½oz) hazelnuts, cut in half

Top tips

• Toast the nuts under the grill for 2 minutes before you stir them into the dough mixture.

• Wrap up a pile of cookies in baking parchment and tie it with ribbon to make a parcel to give to someone.

② Cranberry chews

You can play around with trying the same quantity of another dried fruit. Which is your favourite? Try raisins, mangoes, apples, blueberries, or cherries.

Ingredients

(to add to basic dough recipe above)
- 45g (1½oz) white chocolate, broken into small pieces
- 45g (1½oz) dried cranberries, finely chopped

Top tips

• Mix the ingredients really well so that the cranberries ar white chocolate don't all sit together. They need to be spread out well in each cooki

• Serve the cookies with a glass of milk for each person.

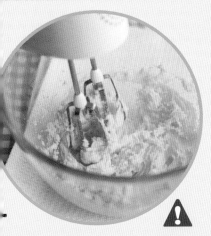

1

reheat the oven to 180°C [350°F/Gas 4). Line 2 trays with [ba]king parchment. In a large bowl, [u]se an electric whisk to whisk the [bu]tter and egg together. Mix in [th]e sugar and vanilla.

2

Work in the flour with a spoon until the mixture forms a soft dough, then mix in your additional ingredients from one of the recipes below. Chill in the fridge for 30 minutes.

3

Roll the dough into about 16 balls and place on the baking trays, leaving space around each ball. Flatten the balls slightly and bake in the oven for 15 minutes or until golden. Cool them on a wire rack.

4

Traditional chocolate

This is a classic cookie that everyone [li]kes. Why not try chunks of milk chocolate or [c]hunks of white chocolate instead? You could [ad]d a twist to this cookie by adding nuts.

Ingredients

[t]o add to dough recipe [ab]ove)
[•] 75g (2¹/₂oz) dark [ch]ocolate, broken into [sm]all pieces

Top tips

• Make the chunks quite big so that they are nice and gooey when you bite into a cookie.

• On a cold day you could make hot chocolate to serve with the cookies for a real chocolatey treat.

Apricots and cinnamon

There are other spices you can try instead of cinnamon. Put in a quarter of a teaspoon of mixed spice or an eighth of a teaspoon of ground ginger. You can substitute apricots for raisins or sultanas.

Ingredients

(to add to basic dough recipe above)
• 75g (2¹/₂oz) dried apricots, finely chopped
• ¹/₄tsp ground cinnamon

Top tips

• Make the apricot pieces small so that they are scattered well throughout each cookie.

• Store in a tin for a couple of days, if they don't get eaten before then!

Chocolate cookies

This is a versatile recipe for melt-in-your-mouth cookies. You can use either chocolate spread for a double chocolate taste or peanut butter for a nutty flavour.

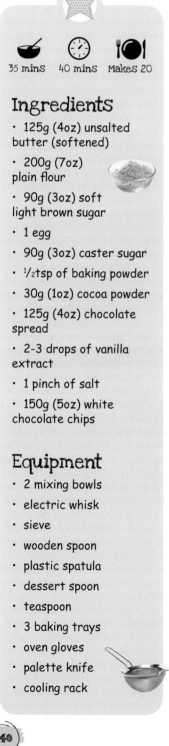

35 mins   40 mins   Makes 20

Ingredients
- 125g (4oz) unsalted butter (softened)
- 200g (7oz) plain flour
- 90g (3oz) soft light brown sugar
- 1 egg
- 90g (3oz) caster sugar
- ½tsp of baking powder
- 30g (1oz) cocoa powder
- 125g (4oz) chocolate spread
- 2-3 drops of vanilla extract
- 1 pinch of salt
- 150g (5oz) white chocolate chips

Equipment
- 2 mixing bowls
- electric whisk
- sieve
- wooden spoon
- plastic spatula
- dessert spoon
- teaspoon
- 3 baking trays
- oven gloves
- palette knife
- cooling rack

Preheat the oven to 180°C (350°F/ Gas 4). Cream the butter and both types of sugar together in a large bowl until the mixture turns creamy.

Still using the electric whisk beat the egg, chocolate spread, and vanilla extract into the creamed butter and sugar mixture, until fully mixed in.

Sieve the flour, baking powder, cocoa powder, and salt into a bowl. Use a wooden spoon to help the mixture through, if you need to.

Add the sieved flour mixture to the chocolate mixture and gently mix them together with a wooden spoon. Stir in the chocolate chips.

5

lace 6–7 heaped dessert
oonfuls of the cookie dough
nto each baking tray, leaving
ace between each mound so
ey can spread as they cook.

6

Bake for 14 minutes. Take
the trays out of the oven and leave
the cookies to set for 2–3 minutes.
When set, transfer them onto a
cooling rack.

Variation

For a nutty cookie, miss
out the cocoa powder in
step 3, swap the chocolate
spread for the same amount
of peanut butter in step 2,
and use plain chocolate
chips instead.

Tip

Milk or plain chocolate would also taste great in these cookies. If you prefer other dried fruits such as strawberries or blueberries, use them instead of cranberries.

Chocolate and cranberry cookies

The perfect combination of bitter cranberries and sweet white chocolate makes these cookies melt in your mouth!

10 mins — 15 mins — Makes 15

Ingredients

- 125g (4oz) butter (softened)
- 125g (4oz) soft light brown sugar
- 1 medium egg (beaten)
- 1tbsp milk
- 150g (5oz) plain flour
- ½tsp baking powder
- 50g (2oz) white chocolate (finely grated)
- 100g (3½oz) white chocolate chips
- 50g (2oz) dried cranberries

Equipment

- 2 baking sheets
- baking paper
- large mixing bowl
- electric or hand whisk
- dessert spoon
- cooling rack
- flipper

1 **Preheat the oven** to 180°C (375°F/ Gas 4). Line 2 baking sheets with baking paper to prevent the cookies from sticking while they are baking.

2 **Cream the butter** and sugar together in a large bowl until they are pale and creamy. (You can use a hand or electric whisk.) Then beat in the egg and milk with the whisk.

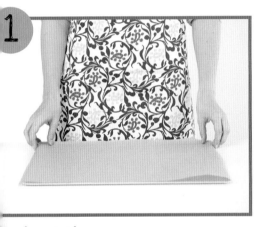

3 **Add the flour**, baking powder, grated chocolate, chocolate chips, and cranberries to the mixture. Using a dessert spoon, stir until they are thoroughly mixed together.

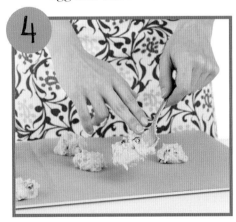

4 **Place dessert spoonfuls** of the cookie mixture onto the prepared baking sheets. Leave space between the spoonfuls so the cookies do not merge together as they cook.

5 **Bake for 12–15 minutes**, until lightly golden and slightly soft to the touch. Allow to cool on the sheet for 5 minutes, then transfer to a cooling rack to cool completely.

Rocky road cookies

These gorgeous cookies are topped with chunky chocolate and melted marshmallows. The chunky and smooth textures are a perfect combination – yum!

10 mins · 11 mins · Makes 14

Ingredients

- 125g (4oz) butter (softened)
- 125g (4oz) soft brown sugar
- 1 medium egg (beaten)
- 1tbsp milk
- 50g (2oz) milk chocolate (chopped)
- 125g (4oz) plain flour
- 1tbsp cocoa powder
- ½tsp baking powder
- 50g (2oz) white chocolate (chopped)
- 25g (1oz) mini marshmallows

Equipment

- 2 baking sheets
- baking paper
- large mixing bowl
- electric or hand whisk
- metal spoon
- dessert spoon
- oven gloves
- palette knife
- cooling rack

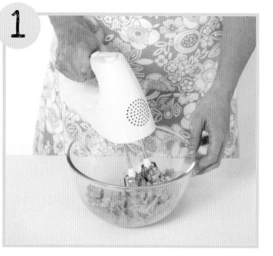

1

Preheat the oven to 180°C (375°F/ Gas 4). Line 2 baking sheets with baking paper. Use an electric or hand whisk to cream the butter and sugar together in a mixing bowl.

2

Beat in the egg and milk. Then stir in the flour, cocoa powder, baking powder, and half the chunks of milk and white chocolate using a metal spoon.

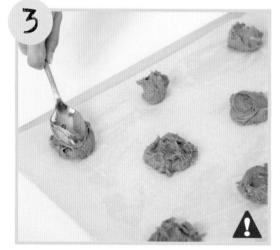

3

Place dessert spoons of the mixture onto the prepared baking sheets, spacing them well apart. Flatten slightly and bake for 5 minutes, until the edges are starting to get firm.

4

Remove the cookies from the oven. Immediately sprinkle them with the marshmallows and remaining chocolate chunks, pressing them down into the cookies.

5 Return the cookies

to the oven for a further 5–6 minutes or until slightly soft to the touch. Allow them to cool for 5 minutes, then transfer them to a cooling rack.

Variation

Experiment with different flavoured chocolate chunks. Or try heart-shaped marshmallows for a Valentine's Day treat!

Tip

Don't be tempted to take the flapjacks out of the tin until they are completely cooled, or they will break up.

Flapjacks

Tasty crumbly oats mixed with sticky golden syrup and crunchy corn flakes make these flapjacks completely irresistible. Oats release energy slowly so you won't feel hungry again for a while.

1

Preheat the oven to 180°C (350°F/Gas 4). In a saucepan, gently melt the butter, sugar and golden syrup over a low heat, stirring with a wooden spoon until the sugar has dissolved.

2

Remove the saucepan from the heat and gently stir in the porridge oats and the corn flakes with the wooden spoon, until the mixture is thoroughly combined and sticky.

10 mins   25 mins   Makes 16

Ingredients

- 175g (6oz) butter (diced)
- 175g (6oz) soft light brown sugar
- 4tbsp golden syrup
- 350g (12oz) whole jumbo porridge oats
- 50g (2oz) corn flakes

Equipment

- large saucepan
- wooden spoon
- 28 x 18cm (11 x 7in) tin
- oven gloves
- sharp knife

3

Tip the mixture into a 28 x 18cm (11 x 7in) tin and spread it into the corners. Gently press down with the back of the wooden spoon to make the top flat and even.

4

Bake the mixture for 25 minutes, or until golden and firm. Allow to cool for 10 minutes then cut it into bars. Leave to cool completely before lifting the bars out of the tin.

Ginger and pumpkin slices

This sticky pumpkin and ginger cake is wonderfully dark and moist. It tastes even better the day after baking – if you can resist eating it for that long!

15 mins   40 mins   Makes 18

Ingredients

- 125g (4oz) butter
- 75g (3oz) dark muscovado sugar
- 150g (5oz) golden syrup
- 150g (5oz) black treacle
- 250g (9oz) pumpkin (grated)
- 300g (11oz) plain flour
- 1tsp bicarbonate of soda
- 2tsp ground ginger
- 2 medium eggs (beaten)

Equipment

- 23cm (9in) square cake tin
- baking paper
- medium saucepan
- wooden spoon
- large mixing bowl
- oven gloves
- chopping board
- sharp knife

1 **Preheat the oven** to 180°C (350°F/Gas 4). Grease the base of a 23cm (9in) square cake tin with a bit of butter on some baking paper and line it with baking paper.

2 **Place the butter**, sugar, golden syrup, and treacle in a medium pan and heat gently until the sugar has dissolved and the butter has melted. Remove it from the heat and allow to cool.

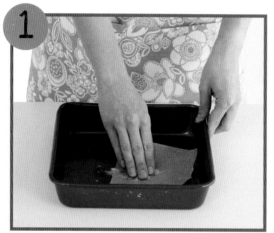

3 **In a large mixing bowl**, add the grated pumpkin or butternut squash, plain flour, bicarbonate of soda and ginger. Mix thoroughly with a wooden spoon.

4 **Stir in the treacle mixture** and beaten eggs until combined, then pour into the greased and lined tin. Bake in the middle of the oven for 35–40 minutes, or until firm.

5

Allow the cake to cool in the [t]in. Once cool, carefully tip out onto [a] chopping board. Peel off the paper [fr]om the back and cut the cake [i]nto rectangles with a [s]harp knife.

Variation

If pumpkins are not in season, use grated butternut squash instead. They have a similar flavour as they are both part of the squash family of vegetables.

Ingredients

- 150g (5oz) pitted soft dates (roughly chopped)
- 125ml (4floz) cold water
- 1tsp bicarbonate of soda
- 150g (5oz) butter (softened)
- 150g (5oz) light muscovado sugar
- 2 medium eggs (beaten)
- 1tsp vanilla extract
- 175g (6oz) self-raising flour

For the toffee topping

- 6tbsp caramel toffee sauce (Dulce de Leche)

Equipment

- 28 x 18cm (11 x7in) tin
- baking paper
- small saucepan
- large mixing bowl
- electric or hand whisk
- metal spoon
- oven gloves
- cooling rack
- chopping board
- sharp knife
- palette knife

Toffee Squares

These toffee squares are yummy!

For extra stickiness the squares are topped with a caramel toffee sauce. You can buy this in a jar but it's more fun to make your own.

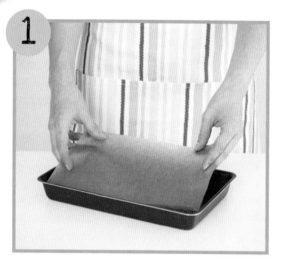

Preheat the oven to 180°C (350°F/Gas 4). Lightly grease a 28 x 18cm (11 x 7in) tin and line the base with baking paper to prevent the cake from sticking.

Place the dates in a pan and add the water. Bring to the boil, then remove from the heat and add the bicarbonate of soda – the mixture will fizz! Leave to one side to cool slightly.

Place the butter and sugar in a large mixing bowl. Using an electric or hand whisk, beat them together until they are light and fluffy. Whisk in the eggs and vanilla extract.

Using a metal spoon fold in the flour, then the date mixture. Pour the mixture into the tin. Place it in the centre of the oven and cook for 25–30 minutes, or until risen.

5 **Allow the cake to cool** in the [ove]n for 10 minutes, then transfer it to [a] cooling rack. When cold, cut it into [1]4 squares, then spread your caramel [s]auce over the top with a palette knife.

Tip
To make your own caramel sauce, bring 75g (3oz) butter, 150g (5oz) light brown soft sugar and 150ml (¼pt) single cream to the boil and cook for 3 minutes, until thickened. Allow to cool.

Chocolate fudge brownies

These delicious brownies are perfect – crisp on the outside and fudgy on the inside. Be careful not to overcook them as they should be gooey in the centre.

🥄 **20 mins** 🕐 **25 mins** 🍴 **Makes 36**

Ingredients

- 250g (9oz) butter
- 275g (10oz) 70% cocoa dark chocolate (broken into pieces)
- 275g (10oz) caster sugar
- three large eggs
- 1tsp vanilla extract
- 225g (8oz) plain flour
- ½tsp salt

Equipment

- 23cm (9in) square cake tin
- baking paper
- medium saucepan
- wooden spoon
- large mixing bowl
- electric or hand whisk
- metal spoon
- oven gloves
- cooling rack
- sharp knife

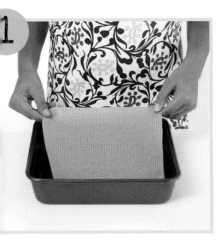

1 **reheat the oven** to 180°C 50°F/Gas 4). Grease and line the ase of a 23cm (9in) square cake n with baking paper to prevent e brownies from sticking.

2 **Melt the butter** and chocolate in a medium saucepan over a low heat, stirring occasionally with a wooden spoon. Remove the saucepan from the heat and allow to cool slightly.

3 **In a large mixing bowl** beat together the sugar, eggs, and vanilla extract using an electric or hand whisk. Keep whisking until the mixture is pale and fluffy.

4 **Whisk the chocolate** mixture to the egg mixture until thoroughly ombined, using the electric or hand hisk. Then stir in the flour and salt ith a metal spoon.

5 **Pour the mixture** into the prepared tin and cook for 20–25 minutes in the middle of the oven, until the brownies are just set. The centre should be slightly gooey.

6 **Leave the cake to cool** for 10 minutes in the tin. Tip it onto a cooling rack. When it is completely cold, remove the baking paper and cut the brownies into squares.

Chocolate & raspberry brownies

These delicious pretty brownies, dotted with fresh raspberries and white chocolate, are so easy to make.

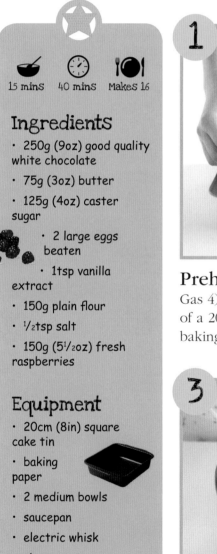

15 mins   40 mins   Makes 16

Ingredients

- 250g (9oz) good quality white chocolate
- 75g (3oz) butter
- 125g (4oz) caster sugar
- 2 large eggs beaten
- 1tsp vanilla extract
- 150g plain flour
- ½tsp salt
- 150g (5½oz) fresh raspberries

Equipment

- 20cm (8in) square cake tin
- baking paper
- 2 medium bowls
- saucepan
- electric whisk
- sieve
- metal spoon
- plastic spatula
- knife

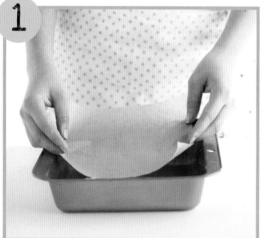

1

Preheat the oven to 180°C (350°F/ Gas 4). Grease and line the bottom of a 20cm (8in) square cake tin with baking paper.

2

Break up the chocolate, and p 175g (6oz) in a bowl and set over a par of simmering water until melted and smooth. Cool slightly.

3

Whisk the butter and sugar together until fluffy in a medium bowl. Whisk in the eggs and vanilla extract, then stir in the melted chocolate.

4

Sift the flour and salt over the mixture and fold in. Then gently fold in the saved broken chocolate and the raspberries.

5

poon the mixture into the tin,
read into the corners and level with
plastic spatula. Cook for 30 to 35
inutes. Cool before cutting into squares.

Tip

Brownies should be
firm on the outside
but gooey and
fudge-like on
the inside.

10 mins   15 mins   Makes 20

Ingredients

- 225g (8oz) medium oatmeal

- 50g (2oz) Cheddar cheese (finely grated)
- ½tsp salt
- ½tsp bicarbonate of soda
- 1tsp paprika (optional)
- 2tsp freshly chopped rosemary (optional)

- 25g (1oz) butter (melted)
- 1 egg yolk
- 4tbsp warm water

Equipment

- large baking tray
- large mixing bowl

- wooden spoon
- rolling pin
- 6cm (2½in) cookie cutter
- oven gloves

1

Preheat the oven to 200°C (400°F/Gas 6). Lightly grease a large baking tray with some butter on a piece of baking paper to prevent the oatcakes from sticking to the tray.

2

Place the oatmeal, cheese, salt, bicarbonate of soda, paprika, and rosemary in a large mixing bowl. Stir the ingredients together with a wooden spoon until they are mixed.

3

Stir in the butter, egg yolk, and water to make a sticky dough. Place the dough on a lightly floured surface and use your hands to press the mixture together.

Tip

You can store the oatcakes in an airtight container for up to a week. Don't keep them any longer or they will start to go soft.

4

Roll out the dough very thinly to about 2mm (⅛in) thick on a lightly floured surface. Using a 6cm (2½in) cutter, cut out the biscuits. Gather up the trimmings and re-roll and cut out.

5

Place the biscuits on the baking tray. Place the tray on the top shelf of the oven and cook for 15 minutes. Remove the tray from the oven and allow the oatcakes to cool completely.

Cheesy oatcakes

These crunchy savoury biscuits are delicious served warm or cold. They are perfect for a snack or a light lunch. Serve them with your favourite cheese and some salad or relish.

Cheesy shortbread

These light and buttery savoury cheese biscuits make a perfect afternoon snack. Or serve them at a party and watch them disappear!

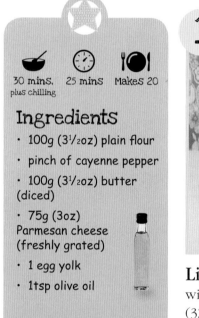

30 mins, plus chilling

25 mins

Makes 20

Ingredients

- 100g (3½oz) plain flour
- pinch of cayenne pepper
- 100g (3½oz) butter (diced)
- 75g (3oz) Parmesan cheese (freshly grated)
- 1 egg yolk
- 1tsp olive oil

To glaze

- egg yolk beaten with a little milk
- 1tsp poppy seeds

Equipment

- large baking sheet
- large mixing bowl
- metal spoon
- round-bladed knife
- cling film
- rolling pin
- 5cm (2in) round cookie cutter
- pastry brush
- oven gloves
- palette knife
- cooling rack

1

Lightly grease a large baking sheet with butter. Preheat the oven to 170°C (325°F/Gas 3). Place the flour and cayenne pepper in a large mixing bowl and mix together with a metal spoon.

2

Add the butter to the flour mixture. Rub it in using your fingertips until the mixture resembles breadcrumb. Then stir in the Parmesan cheese with a metal spoon.

3

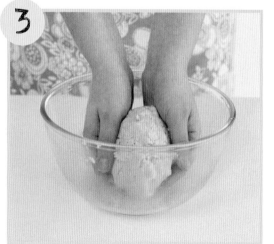

Add the egg yolk and olive oil and stir the mixture together with a round-bladed knife. Using your hands, form the mixture into a ball of dough. Wrap it in cling film and chill for 30 minutes.

4

Using a floured rolling pin, ro out the chilled dough on a lightly floure surface to 5mm (½in) thick. Using a 5cm (2in) round cutter, cut out 16 circles. Put them on the baking sheet.

5

Brush the tops of the circles with the egg yolk glaze and then sprinkle them with the poppy seeds. Bake them on the top shelf for 20–25 minutes, or until golden.

6

Leave the shortbread biscuits to cool on the baking sheet for a few minutes. Then, using a palette knife, transfer them to a cooling rack to cool completely.

BREAD

Basic bread

Making bread is lots of fun, and the smell of baking bread will make your mouth water! This easy basic dough recipe can be made into delicious rolls or a traditional loaf. Replace the strong white bread flour with strong wholemeal bread flour if you want to make wholemeal bread.

Variation

To make rolls: At Step 5 divide the dough into 8 balls. Flatten slightly. Place on a greased baking sheet, cover with a damp tea towel and leave to rise for 30 minutes. Brush with milk, then sprinkle over some seeds. Bake for 20–25 minutes.

20 mins,
plus rising

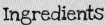

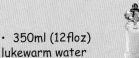
30 mins

Makes
1 loaf

Ingredients

- 1½tsp active dried yeast
- 1tsp caster sugar

- 350ml (12floz) lukewarm water
- 500g (1lb 2oz) strong white bread flour
- 2tsp salt

Equipment

- 900g (2lb) loaf tin
- small mixing bowl
- wooden spoon
- sieve

- clean damp tea towel
- large mixing bowl
- oven gloves
- cooling rack

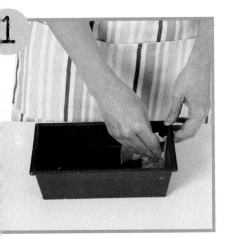

1

ightly grease a 900g (2lb) oaf tin with butter. Place the east, sugar and a little of the ater in a small bowl, stir well nd leave in a warm place for 0 minutes, until frothy.

2

Sift the flour and salt

into a large mixing bowl. Make a well in the centre and pour in the frothy yeast mixture and remaining water. Stir with a wooden spoon to form a dough.

3

Knead the dough on a

lightly floured surface for 10 minutes. Place back in the bowl, cover with a damp tea towel and leave in a warm place for an hour or until doubled in size.

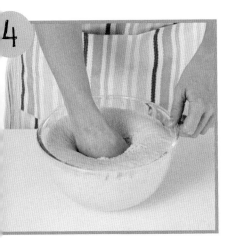

4

Preheat the oven to 220°C 425°F/Gas 7). 'Knock back' the lough, by lightly punching it. This knocks out the large air ubbles.) Then knead it lightly n a floured surface.

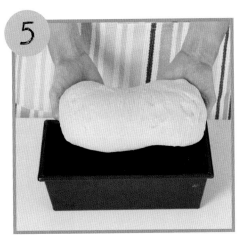

5

Shape the dough into a

rectangle and tuck the ends under to fit into the tin. Place in the tin. Cover with the damp tea towel and leave to rise in a warm place for a further 30 minutes.

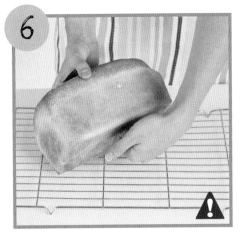

6

Place the tin in the centre

of the oven. Bake for 30 minutes, or until risen and golden. Turn out the loaf and tap the base – it should sound hollow. Place on a cooling rack.

Italian bread

This dimpled bread is known as focaccia and can be flavoured with herbs, cheese, sundried tomato or olives. It's so yummy, you'll keep coming back for more!

30 mins, plus rising 25 mins Serves 6-8

Ingredients

- 350g (12oz) strong white bread flour
- 7g sachet fast-action dried yeast
- 1/2tsp salt
- 175ml (6floz) warm water
- 50ml (2floz) olive oil

To finish

- 1tbsp olive oil
- coarse sea salt for sprinkling

Equipment

- sieve
- large mixing bowl
- large metal spoon
- baking tray
- clean damp tea towel
- rolling pin
- oven gloves

Sift the flour into a large mixing bowl, add the salt and stir in the yeast with a large metal spoon. Lightly oil a baking tray to prevent the focaccia from sticking.

Make a well in the centre of the flour with the large metal spoon. Stir in the warm water and olive oil until the mixture starts to come together to form a smooth dough.

Transfer to a lightly floured surface and knead for 10 minutes until smooth and elastic. Place back in the bowl, cover with a clean damp tea towel and leave to rise in a warm place for an hour.

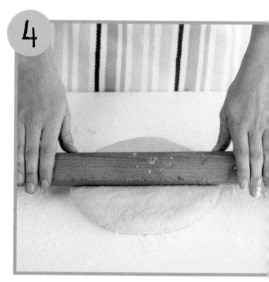

'Knock back' the dough to remove the large air bubbles, then place on a lightly floured surface. Using a rolling pin, roll out to a 20cm (8in) circle about 1cm (⅖in) thick.

Place the rolled-out dough on the oiled baking tray and cover with a clean damp tea towel. Leave the dough to rise in a warm place for 30 minutes.

Preheat the oven to 200°C (400°F/Gas 6). Using your fingertips, make dimples all over the surface of the risen dough and drizzle with the olive oil.

Sprinkle the dough with the sea salt. Place in the oven on the middle shelf. Bake for 20–25 minutes until risen and golden. Delicious eaten warm!

Flatbreads

These flatbreads taste great served with hummous and dips, or with barbecued food. They are best eaten as soon as they are cooked, when they are still soft and warm.

15 mins, plus rising   3 mins   Makes 6

Ingredients

- 250g (9oz) strong white bread flour
- 1tsp fast-action dried yeast
- ½tsp caster sugar
- ½tsp salt
- 175ml (6floz) lukewarm water

Equipment

- large mixing bowl
- wooden spoon
- clean damp tea towel
- rolling pin
- non-stick frying pan
- spatula or palette knife

Place the flour, yeast, sugar, and salt in a large mixing bowl and mix well with a wooden spoon. Make a well in the centre and stir in enough of the water to form a soft dough.

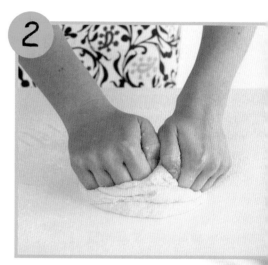

Place the dough on a lightly floured surface and knead for 5 minutes until smooth and elastic.

Return the dough to the bowl and cover with a clean damp tea towel. Leave it in a warm place for an hour or until the dough has doubled in size.

'Knock back' the dough (punch the dough with your fist) to remove the large air bubbles, then divide the dough into 6 equal chunks with your hands.

5

6

Variation

Try adding different ingredients to the flour mixture in step 1 such as 1tbsp of freshly chopped rosemary, chopped spring onions, or crushed garlic.

Knead each chunk lightly, on a lightly floured surface, to make a flatter round shape. Then roll out each piece of dough into a 13cm (5in) circle with a rolling pin.

Preheat a frying pan. Add a flat piece of dough and cook for a minute, until golden underneath. Then flip it over and cook the other side for 30 seconds. Serve immediately.

Sunflower loaves

Fill your kitchen with the homely smell of bread-making. Sunflower seeds are great to nibble on, too, while your bread is baking.

45 mins,
plus rising

3 hrs

Serves 4

Ingredients

- 250g (9oz) strong white bread flour
- 150g (6½oz) wholemeal flour

- 1tsp salt
- 1tsp sugar
- 1 sachet 7g (¼oz) fast-action yeast
- 250ml (8fl oz) warm water
- 2tbsp extra virgin olive oil, plus extra for oiling pots

- 100g (4½oz) sunflower seeds
- a little milk

Equipment

- 4 terracotta flower pots, 11 x 10cm (5 x 4in)
- measuring jug
- mixing bowl

- baking tray
- plastic bag
- pastry brush

Scrub the pots with clean water. Preheat the oven to 200°C (400°F/Gas 6). Oil the pots inside and out and bake for 35–40 minutes. Let them cool. Repeat this process twice more.

Put the flour, salt, sugar, and yeast into a large bowl. Make a well in the centre and pour in the water and olive oil. Mix to make a soft, but firm dough.

Turn the dough out onto a lightly dusted work surface and knead well for at least 10 minutes (use a timer). Ask an adult to take a turn if your arms get tired.

Make a dip in the dough and add three-quarters of the sunflower seeds. Knead them into the dough so that they're evenly spread.

Divide the dough into 4 pieces and place one ball into each flower pot. Cover the pots with a plastic bag and leave until the dough has doubled in size.

Brush the tops of the risen loaves with a little milk. Sprinkle over the remaining sunflower seeds and bake for 35–40 minutes or until golden. Cool in the pots.

10 mins   25 mins   Makes 8

Ingredients

- 50g (2oz) butter (diced)
- 1 bunch spring onions, sliced (optional)
- 125g (4oz) self-raising flour
- 125g (4oz) wholemeal self-raising flour
- 1tbsp baking powder
- ½tsp salt
- 1tsp mustard powder
- 125g (4oz) mature Cheddar cheese (grated)
- 1 large egg
- 100ml (3½floz) milk
- beaten egg or milk (for brushing)

Equipment

- baking tray
- saucepan
- wooden spoon
- large mixing bowl
- sieve
- round-bladed knife
- sharp knife
- pastry brush
- oven gloves
- chopping board

1

Preheat the oven to 200°C (400°F/Gas 6). Lightly grease a baking tray. Melt 25g (1oz) of the butter in a saucepan, add the spring onions and cook over a medium heat for 2–3 minutes.

2

Sift the flours, baking powder and salt into a bowl. Use your fingertips to rub the remaining butter into the flour, until the mixture resembles fine breadcrumbs.

3

Stir in the mustard powder, two-thirds of the cheese and the cooked spring onions and mix well. Beat together the egg and milk, then stir them into the flour mixture with a round-bladed knife.

4

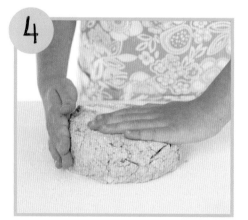

Gently knead the dough on a lightly floured surface to remove any cracks. Place on the baking tray and, using your hands, shape into a 18cm (7in) round about 2cm (¾in) thick.

5

Using a sharp knife, divide the round into eight wedges, cutting deeply into the dough. Using a pastry brush, brush the tops with the egg or milk and sprinkle over the remaining cheese.

6

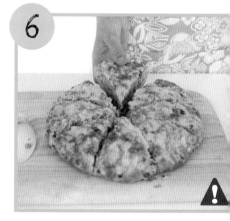

Cook the round for 20–25 minutes, or until risen and golden. (Cover the top with foil if it becomes too brown.) Place it on a chopping board and cut into wedges. Serve warm or cold.

Cheese and onion round

This savoury scone round makes a great accompaniment to soup or salad. It also tastes great on its own spread with a little butter or low-fat spread.

Tip

To make sure that the scone round rises well whilst baking, don't handle the dough too roughly or for too long in step 4.

Multi-grain plait

This multi-grain plait is fun to make and nutritious. If you want to make a white plait, just substitute the multi-grain bread flour for strong white bread flour.

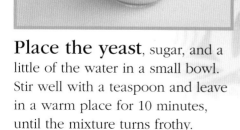

Place the yeast, sugar, and a little of the water in a small bowl. Stir well with a teaspoon and leave in a warm place for 10 minutes, until the mixture turns frothy.

Place the flour and salt in a large mixing bowl. Then rub in the butter with your fingertips until it is thoroughly mixed into the multi-grain flour.

Make a well in the centre and pour in the frothy yeast mixture and remaining water. Stir with a wooden spoon to form a dough, then use your hands to form a ball

15 mins, plus rising   30 mins   1 loaf

Ingredients

- 1½tsp active dried yeast
- 1tsp caster sugar
- 350ml (12fl oz) lukewarm water
- 500g (1lb 2oz) strong multi-grain bread flour
- 2tsp salt
- 25g (1oz) butter (diced)
- extra flour for dusting

Equipment

- small mixing bowl
- teaspoon
- large mixing bowl
- wooden spoon
- clean damp tea towel
- baking sheet
- knife
- oven gloves

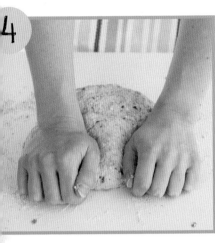

4

Knead the dough on a lightly floured surface for 10 minutes until the dough is smooth and elastic.

5

Place the dough in a lightly oiled bowl, cover with a clean damp tea towel and leave to rise in a warm place for an hour or until it has doubled in size.

6

Preheat the oven to 220°C (425°F/Gas 7). Lightly grease a baking sheet. Place the dough on a lightly floured surface. 'Knock back' the dough to get rid of the air bubbles.

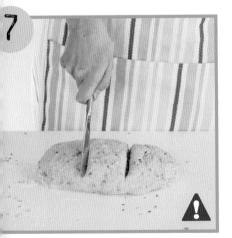

7

Shape the dough into a rectangle, then cut it into three equal pieces. Use your hands to roll each piece of dough into a 30cm (12in) long sausage.

8

Make a 'H' with the dough pieces, weaving the middle piece over the piece on the left and under the piece on the right. Plait from the centre downwards. Turn the dough around and repeat.

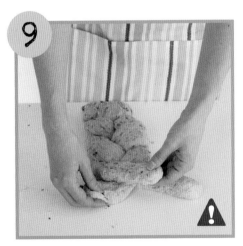

9

Tuck the ends under and place on the baking sheet. Leave to rise for a further 30 minutes. Bake for 30 minutes, or until hollow when tapped. Remove from the tin and leave to cool.

Cornbread

This cornbread recipe is really simple to make and the sweetcorn and spring onions give it an unusual texture.

10 mins   30 mins   Serves 12

Ingredients

- 125g (4½oz) plain flour
- 125g (4½oz) cornmeal or polenta
- 1tbsp baking powder
- 1tsp salt
- 5 spring onions, thinly chopped, optional
- 150g (5½oz) tinned sweetcorn
- 2 medium eggs
- 284ml carton buttermilk or natural yoghurt
- 100ml (3½fl oz) milk
- 50g (1¾ oz) butter, melted and cooled

Equipment

- 20cm (8in) square cake tin or a 20cm (8in) ceramic pie dish, ceramic or metal
- pastry brush
- large mixing bowl
- wooden spoon
- measuring jug
- whisk
- oven gloves
- sharp knife

Preheat the oven to 200°C (400°F/ Gas 6). Grease a 20cm (8in) square cake tin or a round 20cm (8in) ceramic pie dish. The recipe works in either a tin or dish.

In a large mixing bowl, place the flour, cornmeal or polenta, baking powder, salt, chopped spring onions, and sweetcorn. Mix together thoroughly with a wooden spoon and set aside.

In a measuring jug, whisk together the eggs, buttermilk (or yoghurt), milk, and melted butter with a small hand whisk until they are thoroughly combined and frothy.

Pour the egg and milk mixture into the flour mixture in the large mixing bowl. Stir with a wooden spoon to combine all the ingredients thoroughly.

Pour the mixture into the prepared tin. Bake for 25–30 minutes until golden brown, and beginning to pull away from the sides of the tin. Allow to cool in the tin before cutting into wedges.

Tip

Is the tea loaf cooked? To find out, push a skewer into the middle. Then pull it out. If it comes out clean, the tea loaf is ready.

Whole-wheat tea loaf

Whole-wheat flour is an essential ingredient in this fruity, cakey tea loaf. It's super-easy to make, and best eaten while still warm from the oven – either plain or spread with creamy butter.

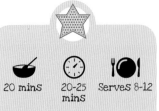

20 mins   20-25 mins   Serves 8-12

Ingredients

- butter, for greasing
- 75g (2½oz) dried mixed fruit (raisins, sultanas, currants)
- 75g (2½oz) dried cranberries
- 100ml (3½fl oz) warm tea
- 2tbsp honey
- 1 egg, beaten
- 150g (5½oz) wheat flour
- 1tbsp baking powder
- ½tsp dried mixed spice

Equipment

- mixing bowl
- wooden spoon
- dessert spoon
- loaf tin

Preheat the oven to 180°C (350°F/Gas 4), then lightly grease a 450g (1lb) loaf tin with butter. Tip the dried mixed fruit and cranberries into a bowl.

Carefully pour the warm tea over the fruit and stir everything together, ensuring all of the fruit is well soaked in the tea.

Then add the honey and beaten egg and gently mix together using a wooden spoon.

Add the wheat flour, baking powder, and mixed spice. Stir well to combine all the ingredients.

Spoon the mixture into the prepared tin and level the top. Bake for 20–25 minutes, or until cooked through.

PARTY TIME

⭐

🥣 20 mins, plus rising   🕐 20 mins   🍽 Serves 4

Ingredients

- ½tsp caster sugar
- 1tsp active dried yeast

- 350ml (12floz) lukewarm water
- 1tsp salt
- 500g (1lb 2oz) strong white bread flour
- 1tbsp olive oil

For the topping

- 300ml (½ pint) passata

- 2tbsp tomato purée
- ½tsp sugar
- 1tsp dried mixed herbs
- 200g (7oz) grated mozzarella cheese

Equipment

- mixing bowl
- metal spoon

- saucepan
- 2 baking sheets
- sieve
- knife
- damp cloth
- wooden spoon
- rolling pin

Put the sugar, yeast, and water in a bowl, mix and leave for 5 minutes. In another bowl, sift the flour and salt, then add the oil and the yeast mixture.

Stir with a knife to form a dough then knead for 4 to 5 minutes. Place in a bowl, cover with a clean damp cloth and leave in a warm place for 1 hour.

Meanwhile, make the tomato sauce. Place all the ingredients in a small pan and simmer gently for 5 minutes, allow to cool.

Preheat the oven to 220ºC, (450ºF/Gas 7). Using a floured hand, punch the dough to knock out the air, then knead lightly on a floured surface.

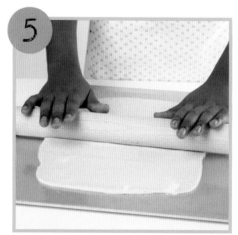

Divide the dough in half, then roll out each to a rectangle on the baking sheets. Spoon the tomato sauce over, then sprinkle with the cheese.

Turn one into a meat pizza and one into a vegetarian pizza. Bake for 15 minutes until golden, before cutting each into squares.

Pizza Squares

There will certainly be a topping to please everyone in this recipe, which makes 2 large pizzas. Why not top one with meat toppings and one with vegetarian toppings?

Variation

Try toppings like peppers, pineapple, ham, pepperoni, red onion, sweetcorn, or tomatoes.

Four ways with pizzas

Try out these classic and new pizzas.

1

2

Tiny toms pizza

This is a classic combination of ingredients and flavours. Restaurants that serve pizza would have this at the top of their list.

Ingredients

• pizza dough ball (from the recipe on page 280)

• 2-3tbsp tomato purée or passata

• mozzarella ball

• 1 punnet of tiny tomatoes

• fresh basil leaves, to serve

Method

• Roll out your pizza dough on a floured surface into a circle that will fit your pizza tray.

• Spread the tomato purée over the pizza using the back of a spoon.

• Carefully cut the mozzarella ball into slices.

• Place the mozzarella slices onto the pizza (slightly overlapping) and scatter the tiny tomatoes on the cheese.

• Cook the pizza in a preheated oven, 180°C (350°F/ Gas 4) for 20 minutes.

• Garnish with a handful of fresh basil leaves, torn.

Hawaiian bites

These are a fun take on ham and pineapple pizza. They'll be snapped up quickly so make sure you try one before they all go!

Ingredients

• pizza dough ball (from the recipe on page 280)

• 2-3tbsp tomato purée or passata

• 212g can of pineapple pieces, drained

• 60g (2½oz) ham, cut into strips

• 150g (5½oz) grated mozzarella cheese

Method

• On a floured surface, divide your pizza dough into 12 small balls. Flatten the balls so they form small circles that are about 8cm (3in) in diameter.

• Spread the tomato purée over the dough circles using the back of a spoon.

• Place a couple of pineapple pieces and a few strips of ham onto each pizza.

• Sprinkle a little bit of grated mozzarella cheese over each pizza bite.

• Cook the pizzas in a preheated oven, 180°C (350°F/Gas 4) for 15 minutes.

Top this...

Check what you have in the cupboard or fridge and try making up your own toppings for your pizza. Here are ideas for what you can use.

anchovies

baby spinach leaves

sliced sweet peppers

pineapple

olives

chilli peppers

pepperoni

cherry tomatoes

3

⚠

4

⚠

Mushroom madness

f you're a pizza fan then this option vill be right up your street. The mushrooms nd mozzarella will melt in your mouth.

Ingredients

1tbsp olive oil

125g (4¹/₂oz) ushrooms, sliced

pizza dough ball from the recipe on age 280)

2-3tbsp tomato purée r passata

mozzarella ball

Method

● Gently heat the oil in a frying pan and fry the mushrooms for 2 minutes.

● Roll out your pizza dough on a floured surface into a circle that will fit your pizza tray. Roll the dough as thinly as you can.

● Spread the tomato purée over the pizza using the back of a spoon.

● Cut the mozzarella ball into thin slices.

● Place the mozzarella and mushrooms onto the pizza.

● Cook the pizza in a preheated oven, 180°C (350°F/ Gas 4) for 20 minutes.

Pizza-pops

These fun lollipop-style pizzas are great for a party or picnic. The combination of peppers and tomatoes is delicious.

Ingredients

• pizza dough (from the recipe on page 280)

• 2-3tbsp tomato purée or passata

• 150g (5¹/₂oz) grated mozzarella cheese

• half a yellow pepper, sliced

• 6 red cherry tomatoes, halved

• 6 yellow cherry tomatoes, halved

Special equipment

• white oven-proof sticks

Method

● Divide your pizza dough into 12 small balls. Flatten the balls so they form small circles that are approximately 8cm (3in) in diameter. Insert a stick into each uncooked dough circle.

● Spread the tomato purée over the circles using the back of a spoon.

● Decorate with grated mozzarella, peppers, and tomatoes.

● Cook the pizzas in a preheated oven, 180°C (350°F/Gas 4) for 15 minutes.

Mini-burgers

These mini-burgers are hard to beat. Make them for your family and friends. They'll soon be asking you when you're going to make them again!

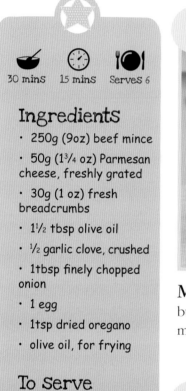

30 mins   15 mins   Serves 6

Ingredients

- 250g (9oz) beef mince
- 50g (1¾ oz) Parmesan cheese, freshly grated
- 30g (1 oz) fresh breadcrumbs
- 1½ tbsp olive oil
- ½ garlic clove, crushed
- 1tbsp finely chopped onion
- 1 egg
- 1tsp dried oregano
- olive oil, for frying

To Serve

- 16 mini bread rolls
- 2 tomatoes, thinly sliced
- lettuce leaves
- 400g (14 oz) jar of good quality tomato sauce or salsa

Equipment

- large mixing bowl
- baking tray
- frying pan
- flipper
- bread knife

1

Mix all the ingredients for the burgers in a bowl. Use your hands to mix everything well.

2

Form the mixture into balls and then flatten them. Chill the meatballs in the fridge for 30 minutes. Wash your hands well.

3

Fry the burgers on a medium heat. Make sure the meat is cooked through by putting a fork in and checking the juice is clear.

4

Carefully cut the rolls in half. Fill each roll with a cooked burger, a tomato slice, a lettuce leaf, and tomato sauce.

Tip

You can decorate your mini-burgers before serving them. Make flags out of coloured strips of paper.

Cheese and pesto straws

Flavoured with pesto and cheese, these light crisp straws are perfect for dipping.

25 mins   15 mins   Makes 30

Ingredients

- 200g (7oz) plain flour
- 125g (4½oz) chilled butter, cut into small cubes
- 50g (2oz) Gruyère or Cheddar cheese, finely grated
- 50g (2oz) Parmesan cheese, finely grated
- 1 whole medium egg, plus 1 yolk
- 30ml (2tbsp) pesto sauce (either red or green)

Equipment

- sieve
- mixing bowl
- metal spoon
- rolling pin
- knife
- baking paper
- baking sheet
- cooling rack

1

Preheat the oven to 180°C (350°F/Gas 4). Sift the flour into a bowl with a pinch of salt. Add the butter and rub in until it looks like fine breadcrumbs.

2

Stir in 75g (3oz) of the cheeses. Beat together the egg and egg yolk and stir into the flour with the pesto sauce. Mix to a dough.

3

The mixture should be of the consistency where you can roll it into a ball.

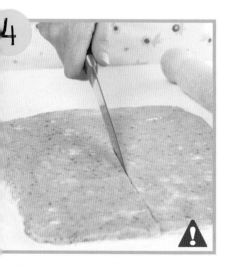

4

Roll out on a lightly floured surface into a rectangle about 28 x 23cm (11 x 9in). Cut in half down the longest length, then cut each into about 15 straws.

5

Line a baking sheet with baking paper. Transfer the straws to the baking sheet, leaving a gap between each.

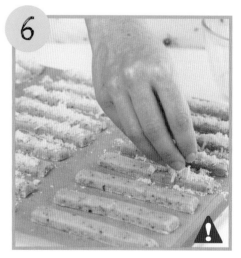

6

Sprinkle over the remaining cheese and chill for 15 minutes. Bake for 12 to 15 minutes. Cool for 5 minutes on the sheet, then transfer to a cooling rack.

Tip

Keep your eye on the crisps as they cook and remove them from the oven when they turn golden. Cool on a wire rack.

Potato and carrot crisps

Use potatoes and carrots to make delicious oven-baked crisps. Once you've made these, experiment with other vegetables like parsnips and beetroot.

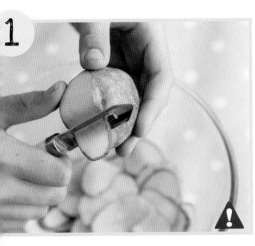

1

Preheat the oven to 180°C (350°F/ Gas 4). For the potato crisps, slice the potatoes using a peeler. Mix them with the oil, salt, pepper, and paprika, if using.

2

Line a baking tray with greaseproof paper and arrange the potato slices in a single layer. Cook for 10 minutes, turn them over, and cook for a further 10 minutes.

3

For the carrot crisps, use a vegetable peeler to thinly slice the carrots. Mix them with the oil, honey, salt, and pepper.

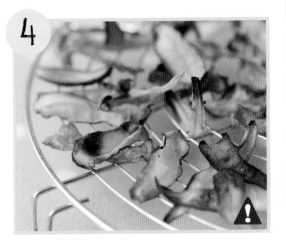

4

Line a baking tray with greaseproof paper. Arrange the carrots in a single layer and cook for 10 minutes. Turn the crisps over and cook for a further 7-10 minutes.

20 mins   40 mins

Ingredients for the potato crisps

- 2 medium potatoes
- 2tsp sunflower oil
- salt and pepper
- 1-2tsp paprika (optional)

For the carrot crisps

- 2 medium carrots
- 2tsp sunflower oil
- 2tsp clear honey
- salt and pepper

Equipment

- vegetable peeler
- mixing bowl
- baking tray
- greaseproof paper
- cooling rack

Vegetable platter

 20 mins   Serves 4

Ingredients

- 1 cucumber
- 2 celery sticks
- 1 red pepper, deseeded
- 1 yellow pepper, deseeded
- 2 carrots
- 4 baby gem lettuce leaves
- 8 cherry tomatoes
- 4 broccoli florets

Sour cream and chive dip

- 8tbsp sour cream
- 3tbsp fresh chives, chopped
- 2tsp lemon juice

Yoghurt and mint dip

- 250g (9oz) natural yoghurt
- ½ cucumber, grated
- 2tsp dried mint

Equipment

- sharp knife
- chopping board
- 8 colourful cups and tray/platter (to serve vegetables in)
- 2 small glass bowls
- 2 tablespoons

This healthy and colourful snack works well for any occasion or as a side dish to accompany a light meal.

Carefully slice the cucumber, celery sticks, peppers, and carrots into thin strips.

Place the vegetable sticks lettuce leaves, cherry tomatoes, and broccoli florets into colourful cups on a tray and set aside.

Mix the sour cream, chives, and lemon juice in a small glass bowl. Pour into a colourful cup to serve.

In another small glass bowl mix the natural yoghurt, grated cucumber, and dried mint together. Taste and season with salt and pepper. Serve in a colourful cup.

Alternatives

There are plenty of other vegetables and dips you can try out for a vegetable platter. So, why not try out green beans and sugar snap peas and a guacamole dip?

Dips and dippers

These dips are quick to make when you want something tasty to snack on while you're waiting for the main meal, for friends to arrive, or for the barbecue to get hot.

Guacamole

Use only ripe avocados. To check, hold one in the palm of your hand and squeeze gently – it should give slightly.

Ingredients

This recipe is for 6 people. It takes 10 minutes to prepare.

- 2 ripe, avocados
- juice of 1 lime
- ½ a chopped red onion
- 2 chopped tomatoes
- 1 deseeded and finely chopped red chilli
- 2tbsp chopped fresh coriander

Method

- Use a fork to mash the flesh of the avocados with the lime juice.
- Stir in the red onion, tomatoes, chilli, and fresh coriander.
- Season with salt and freshly ground black pepper.

Tzatziki

When squeezing the cucumber in step 1, drain off as much waer as you can, otherwise the tzatziki will be very liquid.

Ingredients

This recipe is for 6 people. It takes 10 minutes to prepare.

- ½ a peeled cucumber
- salt
- 1 finely chopped garlic clove
- 250g (9oz) Greek yoghurt
- ½ a lemon
- 1tbsp olive oil
- 1tbsp chopped fresh mint

Method

- Grate the peeled cucumber sprinkle with a little salt, and squeeze in kitchen paper to remove excess water.
- Put the grated cucumber in a bowl and mix in the garlic clove, Greek yoghurt, lemon juice, olive oil, and fresh mint.

Tastes great with...

These dips taste great with other recipes. Try dipping potato wedges, chunks of pitta bread, and vegetable sticks (pp290–291) for a delicious snack.

vegetable crisps

sweet peppers

carrot sticks

bread sticks

3

Houmous

Houmous is extremely easy to make. Try adding different ingredients, such as pine nuts, peppers, or if you like spice – chillies!

Ingredients

This recipe is for 4 people. It takes 10 minutes to prepare.

- 400g (14oz) can of chickpeas
- 2 finely chopped garlic cloves
- juice of 1 lemon
- 2tbsp tahini paste
- 3tbsp olive oil
- pinch of paprika
- olive oil
- paprika
- chopped fresh coriander

Method

- Drain and rinse the can of chickpeas and tip them into a food processor.
- Add the chopped garlic, lemon juice, tahini paste, olive oil, and paprika. Blend until smooth.
- Serve with a drizzle of olive oil, a sprinkling of paprika, a few chickpeas, and some chopped fresh coriander.

4

Tomato salsa

A great crowd pleaser, tomato salsa is nutritious and yummy. Use the brightest red tomatoes to achieve the best taste.

Ingredients

This recipe is for 6 people. It takes 10 minutes to prepare.

- 6 chopped tomatoes
- ½ a chopped onion
- 1 finely chopped garlic clove
- juice of ½ a lime
- 1 finely chopped and deseeded green chilli
- 2 tbsp olive oil
- 2 tbsp chopped fresh coriander

Method

- Mix together the chopped tomatoes, onion, garlic clove, lime juice, chopped chilli, olive oil, and fresh coriander.
- Season with salt and freshly ground black pepper.

Very berry jelly

These individual jellies are made using a mixture of frozen berries. Alternatively you could just use one type of berry, such as frozen raspberries or blueberries.

5 mins

3 hrs setting

Makes 4

Ingredients
- 135g (5oz) pack of raspberry or blackcurrant flavour jelly
- 150g (5½oz) mixed frozen berries

Equipment
- heatproof jug
- spoon
- jelly moulds

1
Place the jelly into a measuring jug and pour over 300ml (½pt) boiling water. Stir until the jelly has dissolved.

2
Stir the fruit into the jug. Top up with cold water to make 600ml (1pt), if necessary.

3
Spoon the mixture between one large jelly mould or four individual moulds and place in the fridge for about 3 hours until set.

Tip

Using frozen berries prevents them from floating to the top.

Variation

You can also serve your ice cream with chocolate sauce or pieces.

Ice cream

Pour, mix, and shake your way through this recipe to make a delicious and refreshing ice cream. This frozen dessert doesn't have to go in the freezer!

12 mins   Serves 2

Ingredients

- ½tbsp sugar
- 120ml (4fl oz) milk
- 120ml (4fl oz) double cream
- ¼tsp vanilla extract
- 900g (2lb) ice cubes
- 7tbsp coarse salt
- mixed berries (optional)

Equipment

- 2 resealable bags, 1 bigger than the other
- whisk
- mixing bowl
- wooden spoon
- clean tea towel

1

Whisk the sugar, milk, double cream, and vanilla in a bowl. Pour the mixture into a resealable bag, close it, and set aside.

2

Put the ice cubes into a large bowl and pour the coarse salt over the ice.

3

Fill a large resealable bag halfway with ice cubes. Place the sealed bag of cream mixture into the bag of ice.

4

Fill up the rest of the large bag with ice cubes and close it.

5

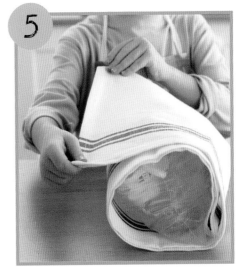

Wrap the large bag in a towel and shake for 10 minutes or until the cream mixture has become a solid. Serve straight away.

Lemonade lollies

Keep cool on a hot summer's day with the zingy taste
of your juicy lemons. Lemons add flavour to fish and salads as well.

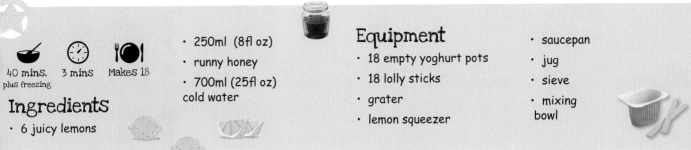

40 mins, plus freezing   3 mins   Makes 18

Ingredients

- 6 juicy lemons

- 250ml (8fl oz) runny honey
- 700ml (25fl oz) cold water

Equipment

- 18 empty yoghurt pots
- 18 lolly sticks
- grater
- lemon squeezer

- saucepan
- jug
- sieve
- mixing bowl

1

Finely grate the zest from [al]l of the lemons and place in a [p]an with the honey and 500ml [(]18fl oz) water. Bring to the boil, [t]hen remove from heat.

2

Squeeze the juice from all of the lemons. Pour into a jug. This should give you about 200-250ml (7-8fl oz) of juice.

3

Strain the honey and lemon water through a sieve into a bowl. Pour in some of the lemon juice. Stir and taste. Add more juice until it tastes right.

4

Leave the lemonade to cool [i]n the fridge. Add the rest of the [w]ater to dilute. Stir, then pour into [1]8 empty yoghurt pots. Place in the [f]reezer until partly set.

5

Push a lolly stick into each pot. Return the pots to the freezer until the lemonade becomes completely solid.

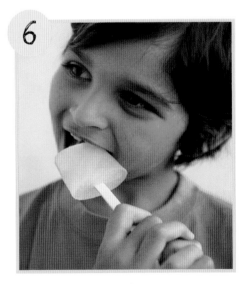

6

Crunch! Enjoy the cold juicy taste, but be quick as your lolly will quickly start to melt on a warm day.

Index

Photography: Will Heap, Lisa Linder, Dave King, Howard Shooter, Craig Robertson; **Home economist:** Katherine Ibbs, Aya Nishimura, Paul Jackman, Kate Blinman, Katy Greenwood, Denise Smart; **Assistant home economists:** Lisa Harrison, Sarah Tildesley, Fergal Connolly; **Food stylists:** Suzie Harrison, Denise Smart, Annie Nichols, **Illustrations:** Takashi Mifune, Malting Partnership, Hennie Haworth, Rosie Scott; **Consultant:** Jill Bloomfield, Nicola Graimes, Denise Smart, Maggie Mayhew, Donald R. Franceschetti; **RHS consultant:** Simon Maughan; **Models:** Max Moore, Roberto Barney Allen, Fiona Lock, Peter Lock, Serena Patel, Christian Rivas-Lastic, Eva Rose Menzie, Ella Menzie, Omid Alavi, George Arnold, Alexander Whillock, Cherry Cameron, Sophia Zeynep, Christian Hannah, Solly, Fiona, Molly; **Recipe testing:** Jan Stevens; **Index:** Hilary Bird; **Garden care:** Capel Manor College.

About the authors

Jill Bloomfield is the creator of cooking consulting company, Picky Eaters. Originally a micro-business that provided hands-on children's cooking parties, Picky Eaters evolved as the "kids in the kitchen" trend caught fire.

Katherine Ibbs is an experienced home economist and food stylist. A believer in the importance of learning about cooking from an early age, she has taught cooking classes for kids and contributed to numerous children's cookbooks.

Nicola Graimes is an award-winning cookery and food writer. She is keen to show that eating well not only influences the health of our bodies and minds, but can be delicious and fun too.

Denise Smart has been a prolific recipe writer for the past 15 years. Her experience as a photographic home economist and food stylist has seen her work published nationally and internationally.